Beautiful grounds & lodging.

"The Great Escape"

Out of this w[orld]

!

ABSOLUTELY Perfect

Bellissimo:

Awesome !

A gem!,

Bloody Good!

GOOT

Superb!

Wonderfully elegant!!

Exceptional!!
.. So gracious

Enchanting!

Heavenly

Great

Leuke Plek!

Fancy and Fun!

One of the nicest places on earth!

What a Treat!

So good!

incredible!

very very nice enjoyed every minute

lovely!

Wat een fantastische plaats voor een weekende weg van alles!

Wow!

Great Views!

Charming —

This is why we love Charlottesville!

Sumptuous!!

wonderful 5th anniversary trip!

SOOOOPER ?

This is it!

Unrivaled

THIS IS PARADISE!!!

Still Terrific

More than we imagined!

また来ます。

Very RELAXING

THE STORY OF

Keswick Hall

Patricia Castelli

Paper Shoe Press
Charlottesville, Virginia

To Terry and Ben,
Till next time when
we can do a tour together
and share what's not
in the book ☺

Best wishes,
Patricia Castelli
June 24, 2016

Paper Shoe Press, LLC
Charlottesville, Virginia

The Story of Keswick Hall
by Patricia Castelli
copyright 2011 Paper Shoe Press, LLC
Second printing 2014

Front cover photo by Jen Fariello, Charlottesville, Virginia
Back cover photo courtesy of Harriet & Dan Mohler
Cover and endpaper design by Sara Augustine, Kihei, Hawaii
Page design by Drew Machat, Berkeley, California
Illustrations and photographs used with permission
Printed and bound in China

ISBN 978-0-615-44469-7

This map of the Keswick area, including the Country Club (now Keswick Hall and Golf Club) and many of the long-established farms and estates, appeared in a cookbook produced by the Grace Episcopal Church in 1971. (Courtesy of Kim Gibbs and Grace Episcopal Church.)

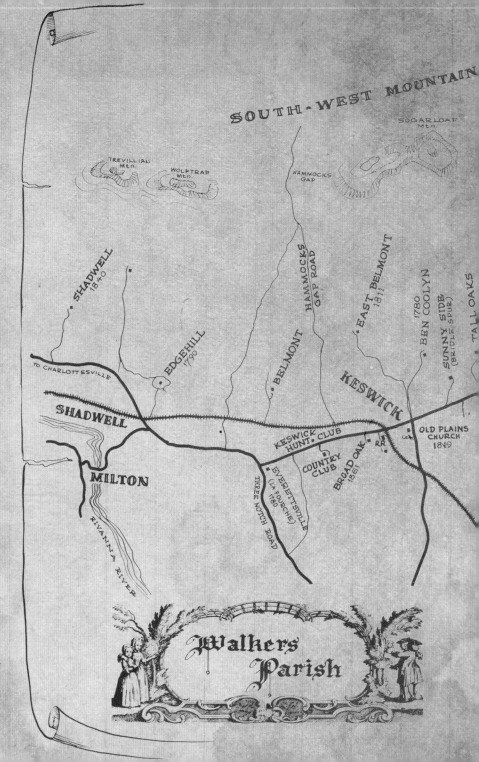

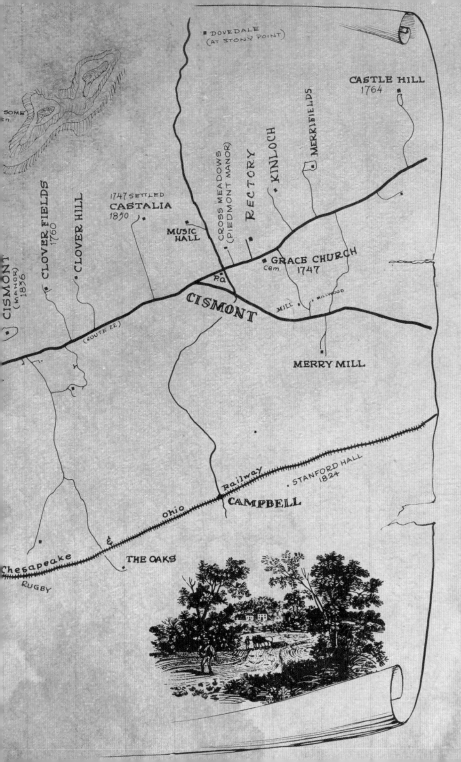

Table of Contents

Mrs. Lizzie Florence Olney Crawford and her twin sons, Robert and Thomas, in 1914, standing in Villa Crawford, which she and her husband Bob built in Keswick in 1912. (Photo courtesy of Holsinger Studio Collection #9862, UVa Special Collections.)

Foreword

"Can you tell us anything about the history of this place?" Guests of the hotel frequently ask this question as they enjoy their coffee in Villa Crawford or as they meander through the gardens or stare at the view from the terrace. Needing some kind of answer to this question in 2008 led me to ask Bob Reid what he remembered. Mr. Reid had been the country club's tennis pro from the mid 1960s to the early 1970s, and one day he kindly shared not only his memories but also many photos and newspaper articles to help me begin putting the pieces together. Thus began my journey of discovering and documenting the story of this property.

Turns out the story is complicated and left me with more questions than I started with. Why did Mr. Crawford leave? Whatever happened to the enormous painting of Mrs. Crawford, or to the boys' miniature donkeys? Where was the second barn? How might the story have been different if go-getter Leighton Kramer had taken up residence instead of going west? Did Mrs. Nelson leave the gilt mirror behind, or not? Did a fire destroy Broad Oak? What happened to the 99 columns, and when, and why was one still standing in the late 1960s? How did that cedar tree survive ? What is Miss Heid hiding? How good was the food during the country club days, really?

Sometimes the story is surprising: Bob Crawford found dead in his hotel room in 1919?! Say it isn't so! Sometimes it's heartwarming: Nancy Root met the love of her life at the Keswick Club swim ballet rehearsals in 1951. Sometimes it's terribly sad: Plane crash, 1953, or Knox Turnbull's death, 1971. Sometimes it's wrong: The golf course first opened in 1949, not 1939. Within these pages, there are other elements of surprise, warmth, and sadness, as well as, despite my best efforts, probably also mistakes.

Sometimes the story cannot be told. There are definitely gaps here: some inevitable because sometimes people don't want to talk, some intentional because not everything belongs in a book, and some unavoidable because either there was nothing to substantiate the story or it did not cross my path or there was simply no room for it. In the end, this book is a snapshot, just a piece of the many conversations about the history of this amazing property. There are more voices to be heard, more stories yet to come – both old and new. I invite you to tell your own (see storyofkeswick.com). Better yet, make new ones. The history continues.

Introduction

A Grand Footprint

In plain or fancy handwriting, guests of Keswick Hall have summed up their experiences using superlatives like *Fabulous! Breathtaking! One of the nicest places on earth! Exquisite! Wonderfully elegant! Spectacular! THIS IS PARADISE! Beyond Belief!* and *simply the best*. Surely with past and present descriptors such as these, taken from the huge guest books on display in the entrance hall and a continual stream of comment cards, Keswick Hall must not only be an extraordinary, must-visit, and will-be-back kind of place – it must also have a lot of interesting stories to tell. Walk the grounds, examine the architecture, touch the woodwork, listen for sounds of the past. The stories that weave together to create the property's collective, cultural tapestry reach into its corners, up and down its stairs, in and among its gardens, and beyond its walls and boundary markers. The stories reach into the past and embrace the present.

This area of Virginia, which the King of England granted to prominent citizens before the American Revolution, has a natural beauty that is quite enchanting – rolling green foothills of the Blue Ridge Mountains, gorgeous flowering trees and shrubbery, and colorful changing seasons including soft snowy winter days and lovely lazy summer days. The thriving Keswick Hunt Club is here, dating to 1896, as well as expansive farms where thoroughbreds are born and raised, numerous vineyards producing world-class reds and whites, and trains still tooting in the background. The homes of three United States Presidents, located within a day's ride of each other by horseback, remain in the vicinity: Thomas Jefferson's Monticello, James Madison's Montpelier, and James Monroe's Ash Lawn. In 1835, Virginia Governor James Barbour wrote, "I feel no hesitation in declaring that I deem [this area] the most desirous abode I have ever seen."

Keswick Hall, in the midst of this glorious countryside, is truly a world apart. Many who have discovered what has made it famous are famous in their own right. In his heyday, Arthur Ashe played an exhibition tennis match on one of the original courts. Alan Alda and Carol Burnett filmed parts of *The Four Seasons* in the original mansion. Lady Margaret Thatcher posed with staff in the "morning room" during one of her visits. Paul Newman and Joanne Woodward loved Room 9, the original master bedroom. Mick Jagger loved the rock fish entree when he ate in Fossett's. The Secret Service enjoyed the spectacular views while standing sentry on the terraces. Anthony Hopkins stayed at the hotel during the filming of *Hannibal*. Donnatella Versace created her own work-out gym in Room 1. Morgan Freeman graciously acknowledged the porter at the elegant front entrance. Robert Duvall has enjoyed Villa Lunch now and then.

Against this backdrop, the stories of Keswick Hall are mostly the stories of people whose names are *not* well known – people who have come from around the corner, around the country, and around the world. Undoubtedly a great place to be a guest, it was and is

During one of her visits, this one in 1996, Lady Margaret Thatcher posed with managers in the morning room (now Fossett's bar). Standing (left to right): Jim Blake, Jim Stackhouse, Stephen Beaumont, Margaret Thatcher, Rick Small, Jean Francois Legault, David Taylor. Seated (left to right): John Heywood, Lara Durkin, Dan Abrashoff, Robert Eanes. (Photo courtesy of Lynne Brubaker.)

Room 9, the original master bedroom of the Villa Crawford with its hardwood floors dating to 1912, is shown here in its 1990s splendor. Phyllis Koch individually decorated all 48 guest rooms in the hotel using Laura Ashley fabrics and wall coverings, many of which were offered only in Europe and only in the designer line. (Photo by Philip Beaurline.)

Club members and guests have gathered at events like these for years, enjoying great food, great company, and an enchanting setting. Here, in 2009, club members and guests gather on the terrace outside the Palmer Room overlooking Keswick's fabulous golf course. In the background stands the same majestic cedar tree evident in numerous archival photos. Behind that stands the Villa Crawford, the historic north wing of Keswick Hall. (Photo by Joe Vaughn.)

When the Villa Crawford served as a clubhouse for the country club, it was often used for special occasions such as wedding receptions. The room shown here now contains the snooker table; the balusters of the Villa staircase are visible through the doorway. Knox Turnbull, who owned the club from 1965-71, stands in the lower right hand corner of the photo. (Photo courtesy of Bob Reid.)

an outstanding venue for special parties, lovely weekends, great food, family gatherings, perfect weddings, afternoons by the pool, and tennis and golf to your heart's content. Over the years, it was also owned, run, and staffed by people who dreamed big, worked hard, threw the parties, paid the bills, cooked the food, tended the gardens, and poured out heart and soul to ensure that the property had a life that would endure. To this day, guests and staff have a good bit in common: both smile often and laugh out loud; both set longing eyes on crème brûlée more often than most people; both discover the property's special touches, Virginia's warmth, the spectacular sunrises, and the holiday fireworks; both are immersed for a time in its character and vitality; both make memories here that will last a lifetime.

A steady stream of good stories, however, in which things are always improving and the new year is always better than the one before, will not be found here. The property does not have a linear or entirely stellar past; in fact it became "Keswick Hall" not so very long ago. One clue as to its many transformations is the fact that it has been known over the years by many names, including Villa Crawford, Keswick Country Club, Country Club of Keswick, Keswick Club of Virginia, and most recently Keswick Hall and Golf Club. Wearing different faces throughout the past hundred years or so – private villa, local club, lovely hotel – it has weathered exciting inclines, nerve-wracking dips, and level sections of just hanging in there. Mixed in with the grand successes, with the periods of pride when each year truly *was* better than the year before, this 600+ acres of prime Virginia real estate has had, to put it kindly, periods of rest, of waiting, of barely scraping by, of trying again – and, to be blunt, of neglect and disrepair, of sad

The late 1940s through the early 1950s was the first period that might be called a heyday of the country club era. Members enjoyed game nights, luncheons, bridge, outdoor evening dances, and of course, engagement parties and wedding receptions. Betty Francis Betts and Hunter Chester Lang had their wedding reception at the club on November 27, 1953. The bride, known to friends as Betsy and carrying cymbidium orchids, was one of very many brides over the years who descended the grand Villa staircase beaming with happiness. A few hundred people came to the Lang's reception in the clubhouse, she recalled with a smile. "We had champagne, and my father was a teetotaler. He allowed us to have champagne! I don't remember the food exactly, but I'm sure we had things like ham and biscuits. It was great food." (Photo courtesy of Betsy Lang.)

dilapidation, of cracked walls and boarded-up windows, of here goes yet another attempt to make a go of it.

The original 8000-square-foot Villa Crawford, built in 1912, served its first 35 years as the primary or secondary private residence of five different owners – it was an elegant country estate with a variety of notables such as silver light switch plates, stately columns to screen the livestock

From its early days as a country club to its present status as a world-class hotel, brides have found that the perfect venue known as Keswick Hall includes natural beauty, impressive architecture, and impeccable service. (Photo courtesy of John Wadsworth Photography and Vow Bride Magazine.*)*

area, miniature donkeys kept for amusement, a mysterious death, an absent cowboy, a curious case of incompetence, bric-a-brac, and a Russian bride. Its 42-year roller coaster ride as a country club of numerous names and peaks and valleys of membership and drama included a tragic plane crash, an Olympic diver, tea dances, tennis ladders, a $3.75 filet mignon, space bubbles, years of echos, an unsolved murder mystery, haunted rooms, and Hollywood movie scenes. This same, solid Villa

Both of these photographs were taken looking east. The black and white shows the original Villa Crawford during one of the lulls of its history. The back extension with its second story porch was torn down during Sir Bernard Ashley's massive renovation in the 1990s. The early morning color aerial, shot in 2009, indicates the magnitude of his project, as well as his desire to integrate Villa Crawford into the overall design. Note the remaining portion of the old house with its two chimneys visible as the left hand wing of the hotel. (Photo, above, courtesy of Jim Carpenter; photo, right, by Joe Vaughn.)

Crawford, presently the historic wing of Keswick Hall, the authentic grand footprint on a knoll now – *still* – overlooking the spectacular, sweeping acreage, boasts painstaking restoration, baying hounds loping by, numerous celebrities, countless gorgeous weddings, and an ever creaky staircase. The ups and downs that have defined this property throughout its distinctly non-linear history include all the elements of life in their own unique time line: dreams, enthusiasm, love, mystery, energy, tragedy, romance, failure, beauty, dormancy, serenity, heartbreak, excitement – but let us begin with a closer look at the heart of the property.

Chapter One

Villa Crawford

As far back as the early 18th century, Charlottesville and its surrounding towns, including Keswick, had been part of a vital corridor along the Blue Ridge Mountains between the United States Capitol and points southwest. Immense land grants in this "western frontier" had been divided and subdivided, and many homes and farms – grand and otherwise – sprang up in this exceptionally beautiful part of the country. One tract of land, owned by the Rogers family in 1838 and subsequently divided, stands out as Keswick Hall's original acreage.

In 1912 Villa Crawford, a lovely estate, magnificent home, and working farm, secured its place on the Virginia landscape. Originally surrounded by pastoral meadows, fruit orchards, mature woodland, elaborate gardens, livestock areas, and barns and other outbuildings, Villa Crawford has been viewed as the heart of Keswick Hall for various reasons. It is the heart because it was the original structure and retains its integrity, including the original woodwork, moldings, fireplaces, and staircase. It is the heart because it has survived so many owners, uses, and renovations, so much neglect, deterioration, and scorn, and so many people from so many walks of life meandering through it and eating and sleeping in it. It is the heart because the creaks of the staircase and the height of the ceiling and the design of the woodwork all beg the questions: What is the history of this place? What happened in years gone by? Who made memories here?

This black and white photograph of Villa Crawford, a working farm, was taken in 1914, two years after construction. The striped awnings were green and white and the peristyle (large white columns in two parallel rows), seen in the far left, visually separated the house from livestock areas beyond. Looking through those columns toward the north, or from the front portico, residents and guests admired the foothills of the Blue Ridge Mountains. In the 2003 color photo, the classic structure is unmistakable. (Upper photo courtesy of K. Edward Lay, UVa Special Collections and Oz Finkle; lower photo by Andre Maier.)

The Idyllic Crawford Years

Robert Blakely Crawford III, born in Eufala, Alabama, in 1878, lived in Houston before becoming a student in the medical department at the University of Virginia in 1898-99 and again from 1902-06. He was "prominent in fraternity and social life... a man of unusual charm, an accomplished musician, especially gifted as an organist, and of the highest ideals," according to an article in the *Charlottesville Daily Progress* on October 6, 1919. His bride, Lizzie Florence Olney, was born in 1873 in Providence, Rhode Island, where her father had been both the mayor of Providence as well as the commodore of the Newport Yacht Club. She had married William Faitoute Keene at age 23 on February 10, 1896, and divorced exactly ten years later, on February 10, 1906.

The University of Virginia Alumni Bulletin of 1907 noted that Robert B. Crawford and L. Florence Olney became Mr. and Mrs. Crawford on January 15 of that year. He was 29 years old and she was 34. There is no evidence that he finished his medical degree; rather, they boarded the first of numerous passenger ships and traveled abroad as people of means were likely to do. On May 11, 1910, according to the United States Census, Robert B. Crawford and L. Florence Olney Crawford resided in the Rivanna Magisterial District of Albemarle County and had three servants but no children; sadly, they had lost a son at birth in 1909. On the census report, Robert B. Crawford was listed as "head" [of household], age 33, with the occupation of farmer; his wife was listed simply as "wife," age 28, although she was actually 38 in 1910. On August 18, 1910, twin sons named Robert Blakely and Thomas Olney were born. About half a year later, on March 27, 1911, Bob Crawford (as he was called) bought his first 134 acres of Keswick land for $10,000 and hired a local architect to build them a home reminiscent of the lovely Italian villas they had seen in their travels throughout the countryside of Tuscany.

Villa Crawford was designed by Eugene Bradbury, who had trained as an architect in Washington, D.C., moved to Charlottesville in 1907 to start his own architectural firm, and worked locally until 1925. He is remembered as a "regionally inspired classicist," an architect whose work reflected the favored Italian style of American Country House architecture between 1900 and 1920. It embraced the two principal components of Renaissance style: a revival of the classical forms combined with a renewed vitality and spirit. Bradbury's strength was in creating engaging residential designs that reflected classical lines and did not compete with their surroundings.

Lizzie Florence Olney Crawford in her late thirties, taken in 1914 while she and her husband Bob Crawford lived in Villa Crawford with their twin sons. A photograph of Bob Crawford has not been found. (Photo courtesy of Holsinger Studio Collection #9862, UVa Special Collections.)

Thirty-seven known buildings designed by Bradbury still stand in and around Charlottesville. His work remains important to the area's architectural fabric and includes St. Paul's Memorial Church on University Avenue, the University of Virginia Entrance Building, now occupied by the University of Virginia Women's Center, and numerous private residences.

The house was constructed in 1912 for $100,000 as a two-story, 8000+ square foot, stucco-

Eugene Bradbury's 1911 drawing of the front elevation of Villa Crawford. A circular driveway led guests to the stately portico which, along with the 100-foot wide terrace, faced the gorgeous foothills of the Blue Ridge Mountains. The house was constructed for $100,000. (Image courtesy of UVa Special Collections.)

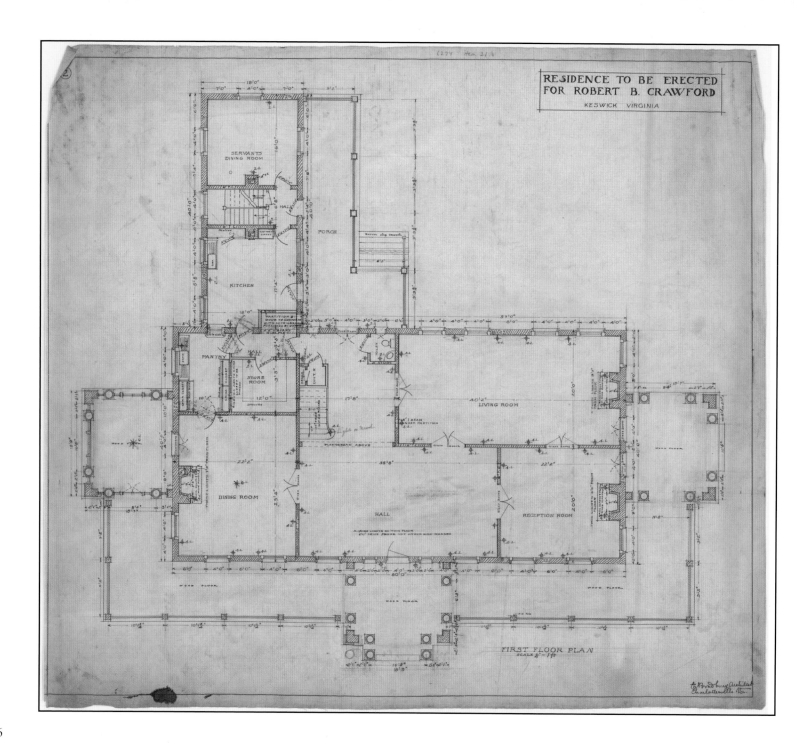

RESIDENCE TO BE ERECTED
FOR ROBERT B. CRAWFORD
KESWICK VIRGINIA

SERVANTS
DINING ROOM

KITCHEN

PORCH

PANTRY

HALL

STORE
ROOM

LIVING ROOM

DINING ROOM

HALL

RECEPTION ROOM

FIRST FLOOR PLAN
SCALE ¼" = 1 ft

clad residence with a tile roof on a perfect rise in the land. A brick terrace over 100 feet long extended along the northern (front) side of the house overlooking the sweeping Virginia countryside and the Blue Ridge foothills. The inviting front portico, still standing and now facing the horizon pool, welcomed friends and neighbors who approached the house via a circular driveway, some on horseback and some, no doubt, in early-model motorized vehicles. Inside the large house, Mrs. Crawford's preference was strongly for silver rather than gold – even the light switch plates were sterling silver. Elegant and lavish were the dinners and special occasions held here. In an article on October 6, 1919, the *Charlottesville Daily Progress* reflected that Villa Crawford "became a social center," and it is said that Mrs. Crawford received dinner guests by descending the grand staircase with ropes of diamonds and jewels around her neck held together, presumably, with chains of silver instead of gold.

The main floor of the house contained the 35 x 20-foot hall, the reception room with fireplace (now the library), the living room/music room with fireplace (now the snooker room), the dining room with fireplace (now the bar), various storage areas, and a large extension to the south (razed in 1991), creating an overall L-shaped structure. The extension contained a second interior staircase, and the kitchen and servants' dining quarters on the main floor. On the second floor was the original master bedroom (now Room 9), with its fireplace, balcony, and desirable corner location providing prime vistas to the north and the east. The main section of the second floor contained a total of six bedrooms, and the extension contained a servant's room, a sewing room, and a built-in clothes chute for conveying laundry to the basement. The third floor (now Rooms 33, 34, and 35) was the original attic of the house and contained another servant's room, located directly above the master bedroom.

An article published on October 1, 1914, in the 'Country Houses and Gardens' section of *The Spur* featured "Mr. Robert B. Crawford's Villa at Keswick, Virginia." Many of the exterior touches described in the article are long gone: the vine-wreathed pergola, the palms that shaded the walkways, the Italian sunken garden, the peristyle of one hundred white columns, the strutting peacocks, the miniature donkeys. But overall, the vivid landscape, haunting charm, and unabashed elegance of the home are undeniably reflected in Villa Crawford of today. The text of the article (author unknown), which follows, provides details of the Crawford's house and life style in a manner entirely consistent with such a report written during this era.

Eugene Bradbury's architectural renderings (hand drawn, with pencil marks on the originals) show a virtually unchanged first floor layout, minus the extension to the south which was completely replaced in the early 1990s. The living room is Keswick Hall's snooker room; the dining room is the bar. (Image courtesy of UVa Special Collections.)

"It is scarcely astonishing to those who are at all familiar with the circumstances that Mr. and Mrs. Robert B. Crawford... should have selected the little village of Keswick in Virginia as the site of their permanent home. What with Monticello, Montpelier, and the University of Virginia group, the architectural character of the surrounding country could not have been better suited to the introduction of this additional link in the chain of beautiful homes reflecting a dominantly Italian note. Villa Crawford, therefore, in the first place, has the incalculable advantage of being ideally attuned to its very picturesque environment.

"Situated on an eminence commanding an excellent view...and embracing a landscape vivid with Judas trees in spring, there is much about the place strongly suggestive of the haunting charm of the Roman Campagna. Two driveways lead up to the villa from the large wrought-iron gates – one through a half mile of apple orchard and pasture land and over a rustic bridge which spans the brook, and the other through fifty or sixty acres of pastoral woodland. Here, in the springtime, dogwood, wild plum blossoms, honeysuckle, wild violets and iris, tulips and hyacinths in every imaginable hue – not forgetting the little blue daisies which the Italians

The earliest known interior photograph of the Villa Crawford, published in 1914, looks toward the family dining room (now the hotel's bar), which was furnished in mahogany and decorated with blue, white, and silver. Unfortunately the "beautiful painting of Mrs. Crawford by Prince Troubetzkoy" mentioned in the article is not visible. The handsome Prince was married to Amelie Rives Chanler and lived locally at the Keswick estate called Castle Hill. Amelie had been married to Archie Chanler, heir to the Astor fortune around the turn of the century, who lived locally at his own estate called Merry Mills. (Photo courtesy of K. Edward Lay, UVa Special Collections and Oz Finkle.)

call "the eyes of the Madonna" – blend in a scented riot of color which takes the dormant imagination by storm.

"On one side of the villa, Mr. Crawford is laying out an Italian sunken garden, which will include the stream and the lake. A series of white marble steps, dividing an avenue of dwarf trees, will lead down to garden seats and a fountain. The latter is now being completed in Florence after Mr. Crawford's own design. A peristyle of one hundred white columns separates the stable courtyard from the formal garden and the house, while a vine-wreathed pergola, box-trees, bays, and umbrageous palms screen the approach to the livestock area. In this enclosure, dainty fan-

The Crawford twins in 1914, Robert and Thomas, shown (above) on the gravel, circular drive next to the front portico of the house enjoying their 32-inch tall miniature donkeys, Tombolino and Bertha, and (right) on the side veranda with their riding habits and sized-to-fit riding crops. Note the black wicker furniture, brick terrace floor, and exterior area rug. One might wonder if the servant in the background is the one referred to in the 1914 article as "the most courteous of Roman butlers." (Photos courtesy of Holsinger Studio Collection #9862, UVa Special Collections.)

tailed pigeons mingle with strutting peacocks. Here also, Tombolino and Bertha, the smallest donkeys ever brought to this country, give signs of being on the friendliest terms with a pair of young steers. The donkeys are a source of increasing pleasure and pride to the Crawford twins. The counterpart of a pair owned and driven by the children of King Victor Emmanuel, they are remarkable for their unusual stature – or rather lack of it; the little animals are only thirty-two inches high.

"Pure white in color, with green and white striped awnings shading each window and all the upper verandas, Villa Crawford is notable for its charming dignity of outline. The wide brick-laid terrace which distinguishes the facade is one hundred feet long. Three upper balconies are supported by white circular columns. Inside the house there is not a jot of wall paper nor a tittle of gilt work. Every wall and mantle is done in pure white and every lamp and newel post light is of silver. Door-knobs, bathroom fittings, portiere poles, and curtain rods are similarly finished. There are few pictures and little bric-a-brac. Of flowers there is an abundance – in Florentine vases of silver.

"A beautiful painting of Mrs. Crawford by Prince Troubetzkoy hangs in the hall, an apartment of some thirty-eight feet in length, furnished in mahogany with tan and blue tapestries. The consols are marble-topped and the mirrors mahogany-framed. To the left of the hall is a large dining room, also furnished in carved mahogany and decorated in blue, silver and white. Glass doors connect it with a tiled, glass-enclosed breakfast-room, which affords an entrancing view of the vine-hung peristyle and sunken gardens. The hangings here are of dull yellow and blue to harmonize with the cream colored furniture garlanded and wreathed with bright flowers.

"To the right of the large entrance hall is the reception room, in old rose and silver. At the rear of the hall, past glass doors, is the music-room, over forty feet long, with hangings and tapestried furniture in pale green. The lofty white mantlepiece

Thomas and Robert (Crawford) Greenough attended boarding school in England; both earned Master's degrees at Cambridge University. Thomas was twice decorated for bravery under fire in World War II, and escaped his captors in Occupied France in 1941; he died at age 41 on November 23, 1951. Robert, who was a Rhodes scholar and earned his LLB at the University of Virginia Law School, served in Air Force intelligence; he died at age 52 on November 1, 1962. (Photo courtesy of Peggy Weems)

is to hold an exquisite marble inset depicting joyous Greek girls at the dance, on which Romenelli of Florence is now working. The artist has also executed a wonderfully spirited marble showing Mr. Crawford's coeval youngsters absorbedly playing with a donkey.

"A square veranda opens off the music-room and joins the long terrace. Black wicker tables and chairs and footstools cushioned in green invite a mild lassitude, and at the appointed hour, tiffin [luncheon] is served in this charming retreat by the most courteous of Roman butlers."

Broad Oak, annexed in 1913 with its 181 acres, was a small, simple house with rough, wide plank floors and hand-hewed timbers. According to a 1987 Piedmont Environmental Council document, Broad Oak was "standing in the 1930s when surveyed by the WPA" (Works Progress Administration); it is said to have subsequently burned down.

Broad Oak: Additional Acreage

Bob and Florence Crawford enjoyed their beautiful home for more than a year before deciding to purchase an adjacent 181-acre farm called Broad Oak, more than doubling their acreage. On August 12, 1913, six days before the twins turned three years old, Robert Crawford acquired this farm for $7500, the description of which had been written by its owner, Edward C. Mead, in 1898 in a book called *Historic Homes of the South-West Mountains Virginia*. Mr. Mead had purchased Broad Oak at the onset of the Civil War in 1861; he wrote that it was so named for the "giant oak...twenty feet in circumference at its base [which] spreads a shade over the yard of more than eighty feet in diameter over the little dwelling as if in protection of its peaceful occupants." Entering Broad Oak "would have rejoiced the heart."

Though it is said to have burned down and even its foundation is lost, the Broad Oak farmhouse, according to Mr. Mead's description, stood near both the South Plains Presbyterian Church and the "little station of Keswick, where the trains of the Chesapeake and Ohio Railroad pass in view daily." In this there is a striking similarity to present day Keswick Hall. Several times a day guests and club members can hear the train whistle coming from the crossing nearby or the rumble along the tracks as they play the 17th hole on *Full Cry*, the Pete Dye golf course that opened in September 2014. Some guests may also recall the train scenes from the motion picture *Giant* starring Elizabeth Taylor, Rock Hudson and James Dean, filmed in Keswick in 1955. But the similarities between the property then and the property now do not stop with the trains. Anyone who has admired the gardens of Keswick Hall, or danced to its music, or relaxed in its blissful serenity may also enjoy Mr. Mead's poetical descriptions: *"Broad Oak has always been famous for its fruits and flowers, which have afforded pleasure and delight to the many who have honored it with a visit. To the young it has often been a scene of gayety, its halls resounding with music and the joyful voices of happy hearts, while to the aged the view of 'the everlasting hills' and the peaceful calm have been ever a refreshing feast."*

The sound of a train whistle is heard in the distance regularly at Keswick Hall. This Keswick depot, built after World War II when the tracks were realigned, replaced the original, built in the 19th century and functioning also as its post office. The newer depot was (very temporarily) renamed Ardmore during the filming of the 1955 Hollywood movie Giant, *about the same time the Keswick Country Club was being renamed the Country Club of Keswick. The Chesapeake & Ohio Railroad still runs along the northern boundary of Keswick Hall's acreage, but depot operations ceased in 1967. See page 53 for a 1964 aerial photograph that includes this depot. (Photos courtesy of Ed Roseberry.)*

Post-Idyllic Years

Happy hearts did not last long on the expanded Crawford paradise. The chain of title housed at the Albemarle County Historical Society confirms that on December 9, 1917, five years after making Villa Crawford their home, Robert B. Crawford conveyed the property to his wife, L. Florence Olney Crawford, with "consideration stated as natural love and affection" (item XVII in the chain of title). On September 8, 1918, at the age of 40, he registered to serve in World War I, as required by law, naming his wife as his nearest relative. He is not known to have served in the war; instead, he moved to Baltimore, where he was found dead one year later on October 5, 1919, in his room at the Belmont Inn – "heart trouble" being the supposed cause. Heart trouble indeed: Some say he died of a broken heart.

Bob Crawford was buried in his home state of Alabama. Legend persists that he walks the grounds around the Villa and has been implicated in certain strange and ghostly events, none (as with such legends) substantiated. According to Donna M. Lucey, Charlottesville author of *Archie and Amelie, Love and Madness in the Gilded Age*, a true story published in 2006 and also set in part in Keswick, "Every self-respecting Southern house had a ghost of some sort. It was part of the enchanting lore of such places." Perhaps Bob Crawford walks the grounds wishing he could try again, perhaps he moans in the old attic from loneliness or mental anguish, perhaps he rocks in the rocker replaying old scenes. Certainly there was cause for lamentation on his part, Mrs. Crawford's own agenda clearly and quickly conflicting with his. In any case, in June of 1919, four months before his death, Mrs. Crawford secured a quick divorce in Reno, alleging cruelty, according to the article reporting his death in the October 6, 1919, *Charlottesville Daily Progress*. The article states that this allegation "greatly surprised those who knew him best. For some years before estrangement, Mr. Crawford's health had been critical, and much of his time was spent in hospitals."

The same article stated: "On her return a few weeks ago from Reno, Mrs. Crawford went to the home of Capt. Platt, an English officer residing near Keswick, and from there superintended the packing of her household and other effects, and it is understood that "Villa Crawford" is for sale at $100,000. Her plan is said to be to spend the winter in Providence with her mother and brother, and to return to Keswick in the spring, build a bungalow, and probably reside there. The boys will be placed under the charge of Prof. George B. Eager, of the University of Virginia, now on a year's leave, who will go abroad with them as their tutor."

Mrs. Crawford did not spend the winter in Providence with her mother and brother. Six

'BOB' CRAWFORD FOUND DEAD

In His Room at Belmont Inn, Baltimore

HEART TROUBLE, CAUSE

Was Native of Eufala, Ala., and Studied Medicine For Several Years at University of Virginia, Where He Was Prominent in Fraternity and Social Life—Married Mrs. L. Florence Olney, of Providence, R. I., Who Secured Divorce in Reno in June—Is Survived By Two Children, a Sister and Brother.

Today's Baltimore News: Said to be a wealthy resident of Charlottesville, Va., Robert B. Crafword, 45 years old, was found dead in his room at the Belmont Inn, 1104 North Charles street yesterday. Death is thought to have been due to heart trouble. Coroner William T. Riley of the Central district is investigating.

As is his custom every Sunday

October 6, 1919 Charlottesville Daily Progress

days after Mr. Crawford's death, on October 12, 1919, Mrs. L. Florence Olney Crawford married Mr. Henry Waldo Greenough in New York City, according to the October 16, 1919, *Charlottesville Daily Progress*, which also stated that they planned to "sail to Europe one day [the following] week." Sailing appears to be a preoccupation thereafter, stemming possibly from her upbringing on the New England coast and her father's involvement in the Newport Yacht Club. Mr. and Mrs. Greenough and the twin boys traveled abroad extensively, in part to get the boys back and forth to private school in England. On these trips – on 24 separate ships' passenger lists between 1920 and 1930 – Florence's birth date moved from 1873 all the way to 1885.

Mrs. Crawford also changed her name. On the 1920 U.S. census report, "Florence O," age 48, is listed as H.W.'s wife with the Greenough surname, though the twins, age 9, are still listed as Crawford. But beginning with H.W.'s passport application of April 11, 1921, the boys are also listed as Greenough. On all ships' passenger lists and school records thereafter, they are referred to as Thomas Olney Greenough and Robert Blakely Greenough. In their obituaries, H.W. Greenough is named as their father. Thus, though Villa Crawford was destined to retain the name of its original occupants, the occupants themselves, after Mr. Crawford's death, acquired new names in very short order and moved on.

On July 3, 1923, according to the chain of title, "L. Florence Olney Greenough (formerly Crawford) and husband H. W. Greenough" together sold Villa Crawford and its 311.3 acres to Leighton Kramer for $50,000, half her asking price (item XVIII). Mr. Kramer owned the property for almost five years, but never resided there, according to an article on April 5, 1928, in the *Charlottesville Daily Progress*. Leighton Kramer "and wife" sold the property on March 26, 1928, to Mabel G. Hanscom and her husband Ridgely F., of Boston, for $38,500 (item XIX), who for reasons unknown sold it six months later on September 10, 1928, to George E. Nelson and his wife Rose L. Nelson, of New York, for $44,000 (XX). At least Dr. and Mrs. Hanscom appear to have made a capital gain. Rose Nelson's extenuating circumstances forced the sale of the property, and in 1936 it sold for $30,000 to Maria W. Heid (item XXI), the last in the string of private owners. On July 25, 1947, the Keswick Corporation, with the intention of turning the property into a country club, purchased it for $50,000 (item XXII).

RS. "BOB" CRAWFORD WEDS H. W. GREENOUGH

Mr. H. W. Greenough, a well known citizen of this county, and Mrs. R. B. Crawford, of the Keswick neighborhood, were married in New York last Sunday, and will sail Europe one day next week. On their return they will make their home this county.

On October 12, 1919, six days after Bob Crawford died, Mrs. Crawford married Henry Waldo Greenough, who had attended the University of Virginia Law School and was admitted to the bar in 1898 in Providence, Rhode Island (Florence's home town). He practiced law for ten years in Rhode Island, then returned to Virginia in 1912, the year the Crawfords moved into Villa Crawford. Following her remarriage, the family took up residence at "Clifton House," on Stony Point Road in Profit, Virginia. H.W. died in 1930 at age 60. Florence died in Charlottesville at age 75 on October 14, 1948, and is buried at the University of Virginia next to H.W. and her sons. In the obituaries of both Thomas and Robert, H.W. Greenough is named as their father. (Article, above, Charlottesville Daily Progress, October 16, 1919)

Leighton Kramer, the Villa Crawford's second owner, ultimately chose his Tucson ranch "Rancho Santa Catalina" over the Keswick property. "An ambitious and wealthy young man with a passion for the old west," according to the Tucson Rodeo Parade Committee, he evidently immersed himself and his household (his wife, two daughters, one son, and three servants – a cook, a butler, and a private duty nurse) happily in their new desert life. He became president of the Arizona Polo Association, and spearheaded La Fiesta de los Vaqueros, a "Festival of Cowboys," held first in 1925 and annually to this day. (Photo courtesy of Tucson Rodeo Parade Committee)

An Absent Cowboy

If indeed Mrs. Crawford "superintended the packing of her household and other effects" in the summer of 1919, went abroad with her new husband, and then sold the property in 1923 to Mr. Kramer who never lived there and who subsequently sold it in 1928, then Villa Crawford sat virtually unoccupied for almost ten years. A wealthy manufacturer from Philadelphia, Leighton Kramer had purchased a ranch in Tucson, Arizona, in 1918, then traveled to Asia and returned from Shanghai on July 27, 1922; he purchased Villa Crawford the following year, on July 3, 1923. Both the Arizona desert ranch and the Virginia hunt country estate would have appealed to Mr. Kramer's strong interest in horses. But he and his family did not settle in Virginia and did not take advantage of its preeminent hunt country lifestyle. Instead, Mr. and Mrs. Kramer traveled again, this time to South America, returning from Buenos Aires on January 21, 1924. Almost immediately they headed west and built an imposing house on Kramer's Arizona property. Ultimately they had no use for the Keswick property, and sold it in 1928 to Dr. & Mrs. Ridgely F. Hanscom.

Dr. and Mrs. Hanscom, Villa Crawford's third owners, resided in 1920 with their daughter Adah and one servant just outside Boston, Massachusetts, in a home they owned free and clear. They traveled a great deal throughout Europe in the early 1920s, moved to Washington, D.C. by 1925, traveled again to Europe in 1927, and purchased Villa Crawford in March of 1928. An article in the *Charlottesville Daily Progress* on April 5, 1928, states that "Dr. Hanscom has begun the work of restoring the property to its former beauty and attractiveness. Residents of the community will be glad to learn that the new owner will occupy it as his permanent residence about May 1." It is unknown why the Hanscoms sold the property just six months later to George E. and Rose L. Nelson. The 1930 U.S. census lists them again in Washington, D.C., but this time they are renting their home, and Dr. Hanscom's occupation is noted as "none."

(right) Around the turn of the 20th century, John Guthrie Luke and his wife Ella, seated, posed for a photograph with their children (left to right) William, Allan Lindsay, Rose and Charles. Rose Luke later married George Nelson, and together they had a daughter, Hope, in 1908, followed by three more children: George, Eleanor and John. In 1928 Rose and George bought Villa Crawford.

(left) In 1932 Rose Nelson invited her brother Allan to bring his family and take up residence in Villa Crawford. In a still image captured from old home movies, Allan is shown here with his granddaughter Mary Ellen, who was four years old when she arrived at Villa Crawford and remembers Room 10 being her bedroom for the next four years. Rose Nelson sold the property in 1936 for $30,000.

A Curious Case of Incompetence

Mr. George E. Nelson expected "to make [Villa Crawford] his country home for a few months in the year and to eventually take up a permanent residence there," according to an article in the Charlottesville Daily Progress on September 28, 1928. Mr. Nelson, the fourth owner, was a Manhattan lawyer whose household at the time of the 1930 U.S. census included his wife Rose, four children – Hope, George, Eleanor, and John – and five servants; their main residence was the home he owned in Englewood, New Jersey, valued at $70,000. But Mr. Nelson's poor health led to his being deemed "incompetent" in 1932 at age 53 and then confined in Beacon, New York.

Rose Nelson, occupied with her husband's care and seldom able to enjoy Villa Crawford, invited her brother Allan L. Luke and his family, including granddaughter Mary Ellen, four years old upon her arrival, to take up residence in 1932. Mary Ellen described Mr. Nelson's condition as "brain fever." His absence did not deter many family members coming and going, hours of horseback riding, leisurely strolls through the property, lawn games in the front yard and lively parties; Allan Luke's film-making hobby resulted in priceless video footage of these activities,

as well as the house and vistas, for posterity. Rose Nelson ultimately needed to sell the Keswick property; she filed a bill in the Albemarle County Circuit Court on June 23, 1936. Included in the sale were "38 chairs, 20 rugs, 2 davenports, 2 pairs organdie curtains, 1 gilt mirror, 9 pieces bric-a-brac, 1 chiffonier, 1 piano packing case, 3 sets andirons, 4 pitchforks, 14 much used auto tires, 17 harness racks, 1 horse clipping machine, and a General Electric refrigerator," as well as the "very large barn" and the "tenant house," presumed to be Broad Oak, which was said to be "standing in the 1930s." Conveyance was made on June 29, 1936, to Maria W. Heid; the chain of title stated that $30,000 was thought "a fair price" as this was during the Depression.

Rose Nelson's brother Allan enjoyed making home movies at Villa Crawford when he resided there with his family from 1932-1936. These images, grainy stills captured from the movies, show his young granddaughter Mary Ellen riding her pony "Patches" guided by "Old Tom" in the driveway that encircled the front lawn (the very young boxwoods are also visible at the edge of the driveway). Friends and family members gathered frequently. The movies show them posing, dancing, partying and playing croquet. Villa Crawford has its outer porte cochere by this time, but it is unknown when this was built. (Images courtesy of Mary Ellen Voci.)

A Russian Bride

August Heid, born in Galena, Illinois, was a world traveler employed by the McCormick Division of International Harvester Company. He described himself as a "machine salesman" on his 1903 passport application, which noted his black hair, gray eyes, mustache, and "prominent" nose. On May 11, 1911, less than two months before Bob Crawford bought a tract of Keswick land and hired Eugene Bradbury to design him a villa, August Heid applied for a passport at the American consulate in Vladivostok, Siberia, the biggest Russian port city of the (then wild) east, and the final stop of the Trans-Siberian railroad, where he had been "temporarily sojourning" since 1906. The passport application stated that he planned to return to the U.S. "eventually." By 1913 he was a manager for his company, and still in Siberia. When he did return, sailing on the "Columbia" from Yokahama, Japan, into San Francisco on December 3, 1919, he brought Maria, his Russian bride, age 24, and their two-year-old daughter Teresa Julia. A year later he left the United States again, this time taking his wife and daughter along for a three-year tour including Japan, China, Argentina, Uruguay, Brazil, Bolivia, and Chile. After a subsequent European tour they returned to the U.S. in 1932, and traveled abroad again in 1935. August Heid was 28 years older than his wife – he was born in 1866, and she in 1894 – so he was 70 years old in 1936 when they decided to purchase Villa Crawford, a fact perhaps explaining why he chose to convey the title to her.

A description of the Heid's home in the first (1941) edition of Roy Wheeler's *Historic Virginia* calls Villa Crawford an "unusually fine country estate, consisting of three hundred and eleven acres," and provides details previously undocumented, including: that the garage for five cars was part of the stable, which had six box stalls; that the "overseer's cottage with a living room, kitchen, two bedrooms and bath" was in addition to the tenant house; that four of the bathrooms were tiled; that there was "a fine stream and gold-fish pond nearby"; and that "although built thirty years ago, it contains such modern equipment as copper leaders, gutters and screens, awnings, weatherstripping, etc." August Heid's great-great nephew Scott Wolfe of Galena, Illinois (August's hometown), has observed, "Quite a house for a machine salesman." The home stood "in the Famous Keswick Section of Albemarle County...

The Crawford columns shown as they looked in the early 1930s, both summer and winter. (Images courtesy of Mary Ellen Voci.)

located seven miles east of the city of Charlottesville, in a community of fine homes.... Being in the heart of a noted hunting section, it affords excellent opportunities for either a private home or a hunt club." An article on July 21, 1947, in the *Charlottesville Daily Progress* recorded: "The complement of buildings on the estate consists of carriage house, stable of eight box stalls, several cattle barns, utility buildings, and four dwellings outside the main house." It is unknown how six box stalls turned into eight.

As early as 1941, Mr. and Mrs. Heid evidently wanted to sell the property. The description above implies that perhaps they hoped the Keswick Hunt Club, established in 1896, would choose to relocate. But no such transaction was in the cards for Villa Crawford. Instead, six years later on July 25, 1947, Maria W. Heid "and husband August" (as stated on the title) conveyed the property for $50,000 cash to the Keswick Corporation, which had been chartered that same day as "a Virginia corporation with principal office at Keswick." Roy Wheeler's third edition of *Historic Virginia* (written in 1947 and released in 1949) stated that "'Villa Crawford,' the August Heid estate at Keswick, has been selected for development as a new country club for Albemarle and neighboring counties."

Teresa Heid had moved into Villa Crawford with her parents when she was 19 years old; she was the only daughter in the last family that owned it as a private home. After Mr. and Mrs. Heid sold the property in 1947, the family traveled a good deal, then bought a lovely house in an established neighborhood. More than 60 years later, at age 93, during an interview in the same family home, Teresa Heid confirmed only that she and her parents had actually resided in the old house. With all lucidity and a bright twinkle in her eye she added adamantly that she did "not feel inclined" to discuss her eleven years of occupancy, other than to say that her mother had been "a very attractive woman." After a pause she added, "Not all Russian women are, you know."

It is noteworthy that the property was referred to as "Villa Crawford" despite Mr. Crawford's unfortunate and somewhat mysterious demise, and despite five sets of owners over the 35 years from 1912 to 1947 (1912-1923 Crawford; 1923-1928 Kramer; 1928-1928 (six months) Hanscom; 1928-1936 Nelson; 1936-1947 Heid). The *Charlottesville Daily Progress* on April 5, 1928, states that "After Mr. Crawford's death the place was sold to Mr. Leighton Kramer, of Tucson, Arizona, who changed the name of the estate

Maria W. Heid, who took ownership of the Villa Crawford in 1936, applied for a passport for herself and her daughter Teresa in 1922 at the American Consulate in Buenos Aires, Argentina. It indicates that she had been born in Russia, first came to the U.S. at age 25, and planned to accompany her husband who was traveling for the purpose of commercial business on behalf of International Harvester Co.

to 'Leighton Place,' but it has always been known by its original name." Two decades later, Roy Wheeler *still* called it Villa Crawford. Between 1948 and 1990, when the property served on and off as a country club, this original name was hardly mentioned. But in the early 1990s when a new owner came along with a grand refurbishing plan, great care was taken to ensure the preservation of this most valuable asset, and the name resurfaced. Villa Crawford it was, and Villa Crawford it shall be.

This black and white photograph (above) appeared in Roy Wheeler's third edition of Historic Virginia *(written in 1947 and released in 1949); the accompanying text stated that "'Villa Crawford,' the August Heid estate at Keswick, has been selected for development as a new country club for Albemarle and neighboring counties." It shows newly planted boxwoods around the circular driveway; the same boxwoods grew considerably over the years, as shown in the inset.*

The Villa Crawford became the Keswick Country Club in the late 1940s under the direction of Mr. Donald Stevens. Improvements included the 100' x 60' oval, steel pool with two-story cabanas facing the original Fred Findlay 9-hole golf course. The original three tennis courts cannot be seen in this photograph, but were completed at about the same time. A brochure from 1951 states: "Keswick Country Club, the newest in this section, is one of the most attractive. The property which was once used as a successful farm was purchased from Mrs. Heidt [sic]. The charming ante-bellum house was remodeled and redecorated, and was opened for members on January 3, 1948. The pool overlooks part of the golf course, and has one of the loveliest vistas in this neighborhood." (Post card courtesy of Mary Jo McCarrick; photo by Ed Roseberry)

Chapter Two

A Country Club of Your Own

In the early 20th century, rural Virginia retained many of its old ways. In the sunset shadow of the Blue Ridge Mountains, Villa Crawford sat in prime Virginia hunt country with its many magnificent houses and farms, and acre after acre of field and forest; it was an area and a lifestyle ostensibly similar to what had been the norm for many, many years. A brochure of that time stated that "Keswick is situated in a countryside noted for fabulous farms, famous old homes, and families which perpetuate the horse loving tradition of this part of Virginia." Many local residents, however, believed change was good and change must come; in any case, the signs were all around. The transformation of city life, demonstrated by Charlottesville's first electric trolley car running on January 12, 1895, spilled inevitably into the countryside. The telephone became indispensible, and by 1922, one out of 17 people in Albemarle County had a touring car or a truck. Donald Gordon Stevens was one of Albemarle County's sons who recognized and applauded the elements of progress.

Stevens was 18 years old when Villa Crawford was constructed in 1912, and had spent his childhood exploring many corners of the county, most likely even Bob Crawford's property, which he would come to know very well decades later. After a year at the University of Virginia's Engineering School, Stevens left the area, and developed skills in diverse fields including shipbuilding and "land sales" (an early term for real estate development). When he returned to his home territory in the 1920s, he thought the Charlottesville community would benefit by having a social and leisure club, and in 1927 he spearheaded and directed the renovation of a plantation on the west side of town into the Farmington Country Club. Through the Stock Market Crash of 1929, the Depression in the 1930s, and the onset of the Second

World War, he continued in land sales, and overall did very well for himself. By the 1940s he was beginning to contemplate retiring to the property he had purchased in Cismont, a small town adjacent to Keswick. But at a party at Boswell's Tavern in 1944, Donald Stevens, age 50, met a woman who changed his life.

Enter lovely, vivacious Helena Brown, thirty years younger and quickly his bride. Their home in Cismont was clear across town from Farmington, a fact that was surely part of the reason he said to her one day, "Honey, how would you like to have a country club of your own?" Stevens' son Stewart recalled that, "The man Donald Stevens was all about having a good time in life." Plain and simple, "He envisioned [Farmington and Keswick Country Clubs as] places for people to have a good time." Villa Crawford, at this point owned by Maria and August Heid, was for sale, and Donald Stevens envisioned another successful club, this one on the east side of town. He gathered a group of investors and set about creating a full-service club for the Keswick community.

"A charter was granted yesterday by the State Corporate Commission to the Keswick Corporation to operate a country club at "Villa Crawford," the former August Heid estate at Keswick....," according to the *Charlottesville Daily Progress* of July 26, 1947, which went on to say, "The maximum capital stock authorized in the charter was $250,000 and directors listed were Richard S. Reynolds, Jr., of Richmond, a member of the Reynolds Metal family, Ray A. Van Clief Jr., of 'Nydrie,' Paul Bloch,

of Keswick, William T. Stevens, of Shadwell, C. F. Dirickson, of Charlottesville, R.W. Holsinger, of Keswick, R. G. Van Clief, of 'Nydrie,' Donald G. Stevens, of Cismont, and R.O. Hall, of Keswick. It was reported here today that the directors would hold an organizing meeting and elect officers early next week....It is expected that the new country club will be opened January 1, 1948. Eventually, it is anticipated that an 18-hole golf course will be included in the development of the property, as well as tennis and swimming facilities."

By August 1947, the club's board had already approved 104 membership applications, with annual dues set at $100, and initiation fees waived for those whose applications were accepted and approved by October 1. A tentative limit of 350 was set on the number of memberships to be granted, a number set to ensure that all members could be "accommodated comfortably." By the time of the formal opening day ceremonies, the corporation had spent $30,000 "beautifying the mansion and grounds" according to Stevens, quoted in the *Charlottesville Daily Progress* on January 2, 1948, with an additional $20,000 for furnishings. A *Daily Progress* article dated February 7, 1948, stated that the Keswick Country Club had had "its formal opening on New Year's Day, which was attended by more than 1,500 persons," but full operation of the clubhouse had been deferred until February 16 due to "contractors' and suppliers' inability to get delivery from the manufacturers" of a good deal of the furniture and equipment that had been ordered.

Villa Crawford itself would do splendidly as a clubhouse with its spacious rooms and prime location. A renovation of the extension off the south of the house was planned to include a dining room called the Grill. However, tennis courts, a swimming pool, and a golf course were also highly important to the overall project, and Stevens lost no time in arranging for these to be made ready as soon as possible. The *Daily Progress* on April 17, 1948, reported that the clearing and grading for six tennis courts began that week, and that the surfacing and equipping of the first three courts was scheduled to be completed by early June of that year. According to the *Richmond Times Dispatch* on May 20, 1948, the contract for the construction of the pool was awarded to the Richmond Engineering Company of Richmond, with plans drawn up by Floyd E. Johnson of Charlottesville and scheduled for completion no later than July 15. The *Daily Progress* reported on February 7, 1948, that completion of the golf course was projected for the spring of 1949, because "it will take most of this year to prepare the fairways and greens for seeding." On May 8, 1948, it reported that the grading of greens and tees had begun. None of the three exterior projects – tennis courts, swimming pool, or golf course – were in

Donald Stevens, shown here with his family in 1953, worked the old-fashioned way to get people to sign up as club members: He asked them. Bob Reid, tennis pro at Keswick Club from 1965-1972, recounted at age 96 his memory of the first time he met Stevens, an ambitious entrepreneur. "Turn the clock back to 1948," Mr. Reid said. "My wife and I bought a farm in Orange County. I was home that day, out on the tractor, and a car drives up. A gentleman gets out, and he was selling new memberships, year-round memberships to the new Keswick Club. Well, we had just bought the farm, didn't have a penny to put into a country club membership, but quite a few people in the area did sign up. It was Donald Stevens himself who came, saying 'I'm selling lifetime memberships to the new Keswick Country Club.'" (Photo courtesy of Rosely Stevens.)

fact completed on schedule. The tennis courts came close; they were completed in mid July, 1948. The pool was actually not completed until the following summer, with a gala opening on May 30, 1949. And the golf course saw its first official round played on June 15, 1949.

The Original Tennis Courts

Tennis in those days was played with wooden rackets, there was no such thing as a tiebreaker, the server had to keep one foot on the ground at all times, and tennis balls were white, as was the attire of every player on the court. The sport had steadily increased in popularity due to the trickle-down effect of Americans becoming prominent players at the world's most prestigious tournament, Wimbledon. The great Don Budge won Wimbledon in 1937, the first year it was televised, and again in 1938; Bobby Riggs won in 1939 (he also lost to Billy Jean King in a famous match in 1973); and Jack Kramer won in 1947 (the tournament had not been played during World War II). Keswick Country Club's leadership planned to play into growing overall enthusiasm about tennis: the courts would be beautiful, and they would be ready soon.

A formal exhibition was staged to "constitute the opening of the Club's new tennis courts," its first completed outdoor facility, reported the *Charlottesville Daily Progress* on July 30, 1948. "Frank Kovacs, number 3 ranking tennis pro, who defeated Donald Budge in a recent national professional contest, will meet Welby Van Horn, who went 73 games before losing to the 'World's Greatest Amateur,' Jack Kramer, at the Keswick Country Club Sunday afternoon at 3:00 o'clock." The announcement of the match in the *Richmond Times Dispatch* of July 29, 1948, packed a little more punch: "Tennis Stars To Play Here on Saturday," ran the title. The article then noted that the exhibition match involved players who "rank just below Jack Kramer and Bobby Riggs in American tennis circles." Tickets were available for sale in Richmond at the Southern Athletic Supply Company and at Harris-Brenaman's for $1.50, plus tax. Spectators were reminded that "There will be no bleachers, only reserved chairs." The match was delayed twice because of rain, and perhaps because of this, tickets were advertised in the *Daily Progress* for $1.00 plus tax, and arrangements were made "for the erection of bleachers seating 420 persons for the convenience of those attending the Sunday exhibition." Another *Daily Progress* article,

Tennis stars of their day Frank Kovacs and Welby Van Horn played an exhibition match to celebrate the opening of the first three tennis courts at the Keswick Country Club in August 1948. (Charlottesville Daily Progress, August 3, 1948)

on August 2, 1948, played up the event further still: "Due to the large interest in the exhibition match between the second and third nationally ranked professionals, tickets will be placed on sale tomorrow at Brown's Gift Shop, Anderson Brothers Book Store, and at the Keswick Club."

Keswick's Oval, Steel Swimming Pool

This old photo of the original pool looks toward the Villa Crawford-turned-clubhouse. Note the overhead lights that resemble a ship's mast, purposely erected to complement the pool's ship-like design, and the cedar tree in the background, which still stands. The pool was disassembled in 1991. (Photo courtesy of Bob Reid.)

As pools go, the pool at the Keswick Country Club was certainly unusual. Not only did it overlook the lovely Virginia countryside, not only did it have two-story poolside cabanas for changing and for cocktail parties, not only did it have underwater lights and special filters. This pool was in fact made from welded steel and designed like the sterns of two ships put together to form an oval shape (sterns being rounded in those days), a design originating with Donald Stevens, who, having learned about shipbuilding in his younger years, had determined to "build a steel pool that has never been done before," according to his son Stewart. Overhead lights resembling ships' masts at either end of the pool were intended to give members and their guests the feeling that they were on a majestic ocean liner. Earth was pushed up all around the pool to stand in for the water that normally surrounds and supports a ship, and concrete was used to create decking the entire way around the pool for lounge chairs and umbrellas. It was one of the largest above-grade pools in the South in its day, with dimensions of 100 feet by 60 feet, holding 750,000 gallons of water, and taking almost 36 hours to fill. It was located 135 feet northwest of the clubhouse's main portico; its side contours are still visible just west of the present clubhouse.

Together with the cabanas, the pool cost $70,000. It was completed in the summer of 1949, and had its own version of a gala opening. Festivities included a beauty contest with 25 contestants, the Charlottesville Municipal Band playing during the buffet supper, and an impressive diving exhibition. The *Daily Progress* reported on May 31, 1949, that on opening day, Miss Danny Nichols was awarded the "Miss Keswick" title from among the contestants, and that Bruce Harlan, "the Ohio State University

Olympic diving champion, climaxed the opening of the new Keswick Country Club swimming pool with a brilliant two-hour springboard exhibition" including "three new dives of his own invention that no one else has ever attempted successfully." (Bruce Harlan won one gold and one silver medal at the 1948 Summer Olympics in London.) About 200 club members attended Harlan's exhibition, which included not only his spectacular dives, but also "a 30-minute comedy set in a Gay Nineties bathing suit demonstrating different methods of swimming and some 'fancy' dives from the board."

A Fred Findlay 9-Hole Golf Course

Fred Findlay, the nationally known golf course architect, had designed many of the finer courses on the east coast, including the course at Farmington Country Club and the James River course of the Country Club of Virginia. In describing the natural advantages of the Keswick property, he is quoted on August 27, 1947, in the *Charlottesville Daily Progress* and the *Richmond Times Dispatch* as follows: "Please be advised to spare no effort to have this a real modern golf course. You do not realize how fortunate you are in having all these possibilities. The natural valleys with lovely building sites between are all that could be desired and where such natural beauty and opportunities abound, it would be a sacrilege to consider any less than a Grade A golf course. The soil is of a very good and suitable quality. Moreover, the lay of the land is wonderfully suited for excellent golf holes with slightly rolling fairways,

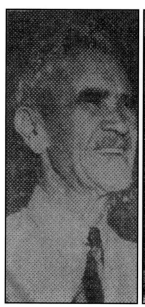

Fred Findlay (left) in the Richmond Times Dispatch, *August 27, 1947. The group photo (*Charlottesville Daily Progress, *date unknown, courtesy of Poppy Paulos) shows the trophy award ceremony following one of first golf tournaments at Keswick Country Club. The original caption read: "W.E. (Rudy) Lawrence, third from left, receives Keswick Country Club championship trophy from Donald Stevens, president of Keswick and donor of the trophy. Looking on are J.R. Ponton, left, golf chairman, and Tommy Card, right, Keswick pro."*

This engraving on a silver chafing dish indicates Chapman Ballard as the winner of the first flight in the 1951 Championship. (Photo courtesy of Edie Ballard.)

coupled with perfect dog leg bends, and the natural contours for greens are absolutely excellent."

A gala opening seems to have been planned for the 9-hole golf course as well. In the *Milwaukee Journal* of March 3, 1949, in a column called Roundup, it states that "General Omar Bradley has agreed to play the first golf match when Virginia's Keswick Country Club is opened next spring and to bring another full general as his opponent. No doubt they'll play with brassies!" Such an exhibition, however, appears not to have taken place. (General Bradley was presumably obligated to rearrange his priorities. No doubt he was sorely missed.) The *Daily Progress* reported on March 10, 1949, that "Tommy Card, 32-year-old Raleigh, N.C., professional, has been named to take charge of the golf activities at the Keswick Country Club, beginning May 1...." and that "The Keswick Country Club will formally open its golf course on June 1." Inexplicably, though perhaps through a simple typographical error, the year 1939 came to be associated with the start of the country club era, and particularly with the opening of the golf course. However, considerable documentation affirms the purchase of the property in 1947, its opening as a country club in 1948, and the course opening in 1949, not 1939. On June 14, 1949, the *Daily Progress* reported, "The new 9-hole Keswick Country Club golf course will open for members and their guests tomorrow."

The golf course became just as popular as the club's founders had thought it would be, and players kept coming. Edie Ballard, for example, was a regular on the golf course. She and her husband Chapman joined the club early on when Donald Stevens had come around to their company, Standard Produce, and suggested the lifetime membership for $1500, which had a provision that it could be passed on to the oldest son. "The course was nice. Two friends of mine and I – we were the three musketeers, and we would play three or four times a week. We'd play nine holes in the morning, go eat lunch in the 19th Hole – and watch *Search for Tomorrow* – then go play nine holes again. My husband Chap played every Wednesday, Saturday and Sunday."

TUESDAY, JUNE 16

Shrimp Cocktail	1.00	Vichyssoise	.25
Fruit Cup	.35	Champagne Cocktail	1.00

* * * * * * * * * * * * * * * *

Any $2.50 item, listed below, may be served for $1.50
with Vegetables and Beverage

Plantation Vegetable Soup	Chicken Consomme
Chilled Tomato Juice	Jellied Bouillon

Assorted Relishes

Steamed Filet of White Fish - Egg Sauce	2.50
Broiled Maine Lobster Tail - Drawn Butter	3.00
Breaded Veal Cutlet - Tomato Sauce	2.50
Assorted Cold Cuts with Potato Salad	2.50
Roast Leg of Lamb - Natural Sauce	2.50

SALAD

DESSERTS

Plantation Buttermilk Pie	Maple Cream Pie	Fruit Jello
Home Made Rice Pudding	Peach Short Cake	Sliced Oranges

Cup Custard

Ice Cream	Sundaes	Parfaits	Sherbets

TO ORDER FROM THE CHARCOAL GRILL

Choice Filet Mignon with Mushrooms	$3.75
Broiled A.A. Western Sirloin Steak	3.50
Broiled Half Native Chicken au Beurre	2.75

CHILDREN'S PORTIONS UPON REQUEST

John Gaines, Jr. was the chef at Keswick Country Club in the late 1940s and early 1950s, and his food was the subject of rave reviews. The menu shown here is one of several that his son held onto. "He was the best cook in Charlottesville," said his son, John Gaines III, an opinion echoed by numerous club members of the time. "He did the menus, and made both lunch and dinner, six days a week. I was 14 or 15 when I worked there myself as a dishwasher during the summer in the early 50s, and walked home from Keswick once – I didn't have a ride – probably 10 miles to home. The club was busy at that time. There was a certain air about Keswick. You didn't have many what we called snakes coming there." Snakes? "Poor tippers." (Photo by Holsinger Studio, courtesy of John Gaines III.)

Fun for All and Romance for Some

The poolside cabanas, available for rent for $100 per season, were private venues for members who paid for the space and could then use them as they would use their homes for entertaining. They were contained within the 75-foot long bathhouse, which also had lockers and showers for guests, and was located on the west side of the pool so as not to block the vista. According to Poppy Paulos, daughter of Donald Stevens, "The first two on the upper level were my mother's. They were combined together so she had a 'great estate' of cabanas at the top of the staircase. They were definitely *ours*. I don't know if Daddy just took those because he was the mastermind of the property – he just claimed them from the very beginning."

The Stevens family spent a lot of time at the pool and made quite an impression. Beverly, the bartender in the 19th Hole that so many club members remember fondly, must have always known when Helena Stevens was ordering a drink. Daughter Rosely Stevens remembers, "My mother used to like to have the waiters bring drinks up to the cabanas – she'd have them put dry ice in the drink so there would be all this haze dripping off the drink." Edie Ballard remembers that "Helena used to change her bathing suit four or five times a day." And Debbie (Slee) Gibbs, whose parents managed the club from 1954-56 and again from 1965-67, recalls, "All the Stevens kids and their mother would parade down there in their leopard bikinis – it was the cutest thing!"

The pool was the scene of at least one true love story. Nancy Louise Hagen was 19 when her family moved to Charlottesville from Glencoe, Illinois, in 1950. "My mother and my grandmother didn't want to move," she said, "but Daddy always wanted a farm. He used to take me driving out in the country to smell the manure. We had a family vote. At that time the University of Virginia had only guys – no girls except nursing students and education – so I thought 'My word, I'll have all these darling boys!' So I voted that we move."

In August of that same year, the two lifeguards at Keswick Country Club had an idea that would make history. Norman Scott and Joan Florence realized that never before had a "water ballet" been performed in the Charlottesville area, and here at the club they had a marvelous pool for such an event. They hoped they could raise money for a high diving board. It was too late for a performance that year, so they set a date for the following summer and began to make plans. They could not have known what their plans would mean for Nancy Hagen.

At first, Norman and Joan had thought about bringing in a professional troupe, but then saw talent right there among the club members. They found nineteen young women anxious to participate in a performance of exhibition diving and synchronized swim routines set to music in the pool.   Their outfits included rhinestone bracelets which would sparkle under the lights when their arms came up out of the water during the evening event.

"Aqua Maids In Review" was indeed quite a production, as the following text, taken directly from the program, indicates.

> *In all theatrical productions, whether professional or amateur, there are unexpected headaches that arise, and "Aqua maids in Review" is no exception. The time for rehearsals was one of the main difficulties. The Club management graciously gave permission for practice to be at anytime. Between five o'clock and seven every night was determined as the most convenient for the working girls and those attending summer school.*
>
> *Costumes were another worry. Anne Baker designed an outfit that was both comfortable and attractive. The problems of lighting, props and music were also finally solved. The rehearsals, all six weeks of them, were long and strenuous. The first week was, needless to say, the hardest. New strokes had to be learned, and the ability to swim in formation had to be instilled in everyone. The rehearsals at this time could be compared to drilling at an army camp, with "Scottie" as top sergeant and the girls as new recruits. Such remarks as "Get your arms higher!" "Reach for the sky!" "You're not in time with the rest!" and "What's the matter? Can't you count?" became all too familiar. In the second week, the actual rehearsals started. The first act was worked out completely. In the next two weeks, the other two acts were also worked out. In the fifth week, the three acts were coordinated. During the sixth and last week of rehearsals, all defects were taken care of and the girls had the final dress rehearsal.*
>
> *The rehearsals were still long and almost as tiring as they were the first day. It was not unusual to find the girls getting discouraged occasionally, and wondering if "Aqua maids in Review" was really worth all the effort.*
>
> *The results of all this work should be evident in tonight's show. We hope it is a show you will enjoy and one you will not soon forget.*

Nancy Hagen wasn't actually in the swim ballet because, as she said, "I didn't want to get my hair wet. So Norman made me the music director." One day during the weeks of practice, one very important day, "I was sitting with Joan on the edge of the pool" (with dry hair, we may presume). The fact that she caught the eye of John Root didn't surprise her. "I caught a lot of eyes

Maxine Ix (above, left) graces the cover of the July 21, 1951, Aqua Maids program, which contains a perfect description of the rehearsals. One page of the program (right) shows the entire troupe of Aqua Maids. The goal of the performance had been to raise funds for a high diving board. (Program courtesy of Joan Tutan.)

43

back then," she said. John Root had moved to Virginia in 1941 from Michigan with his parents. In 1951, he said, "I was at [the University of] Virginia and also in the Marines, and while I was home on a weekend pass, I stopped by here on the way back to camp, and that's where I met Nancy – at a practice session for this water ballet. All the girls were in the water and they were practicing and Norman was there and [Nancy] was there."

Thus Nancy got her darling boy. Mr. & Mrs. John Root had their wedding reception on June 14, 1952, at the Keswick Club. Joan Florence was one of the bridesmaids, and Nancy Root took her place among the many Keswick brides over the years who threw their bouquets from the stairs in Villa Crawford.

Acreage, Plats, Access, and Estate

Most people, including beautiful brides, were unconcerned about the details of the property; they just knew it was a great place to gather. But a study of the chain of title, deed book references, and plat sketches over the years reveals multiple transactions – both buying and selling – meaning that the overall shape and borders of the property and the actual number of acres changed quite often. The purchase of R.O. Hall's Paradise Farm (126.8 acres) in September, 1947, had brought the club's total acreage was 527 and was particularly advantageous because it gave members and guests direct access to the club via a private road off Route 250. In 1949 the club purchased 25 additional acres from the Chesapeake & Ohio Railroad after the tracks were realigned and the new depot was built. The Route 250 access was lost in 1961 when the club was obliged to transfer 21.5 acres to the Commonwealth of Virginia for the construction of Interstate 64. The number of acres rose and fell, but the concept of Keswick Estates took hold. Donald Stevens, for one, according to his son Stewart, felt that the club should "have a residence, a homeowners association that would help support it." The concept in its present form did not get off the ground for many years, but one home was in place almost from the beginning -- a small, white ranch visible for many years from the terrace of Keswick Hall. According to Gordon Wheeler, who lived in the house until 2005, R.O. Hall was "in the construction business and did the roads through [Keswick Country Club].

Nancy and John Root celebrated their wedding with a reception at Keswick Club on June 14, 1952. This photograph was taken in front of the Villa Crawford; its portico is seen to the left, behind the wedding party, which included (l to r) Helen Proffit, Joan (Florence) Tutan, Joanne Manley, Jennie Felton. John Root became a dentist and worked in the area all his life. Dr. and Mrs. Root celebrated their 57th wedding anniversary at Keswick Hall on June 14, 2009. (Photo courtesy of Nancy Root.)

It so happened that in 1951, I married Elizabeth Hall, who was R.O. Hall's daughter. He had given his daughter two lots, and we started that house in 1954, moved in 1955." The horses that his wife kept are remembered in two ways: it is said that Liz Wheeler rode right into the lower-level 19th Hole tavern during the country club era, causing a minor ruckus and a lot of fun, and much later, during the Ashley era, horses enhanced the charming view from the terrace as they pastured in their corral.

One interesting structure built on the Paradise Farm tract was "R.O. Hall's party house," so called by long time resident Peter Hallock of another Keswick farm, Ben Coolyn. During country club days, when this small log house with its impressive stone fireplace was accessible off of Black Cat Road, it belonged to William and Elisabeth Aaron (known to family and friends as Bill and Diz), who had moved into the house in the late 1940s, bought it in 1952 from the Keswick Corporation, and stayed there until their oldest daughter, Elisabeth, was five. The activities and excitement of the relatively new Keswick Country Club went largely unnoticed by the young girls who lived, as Elisabeth Aaron recalls, "a childhood very much in the country." Their experience included muskrats in the pond (long since drained), a collie that kept Elisabeth and her sister Ellen away from said pond, duck pets named Duck-Duck and Pearly, foxes that caused the disappearance of said pets, flying squirrels that occasionally got in through chinks in the logs, noisy hailstorms on the tin roof, a copper drainboard in the kitchen, "boggus" (asparagus) that the family planted, and a kind and patient handyman named Ed. Elisabeth recalls that the Keswick Club was "the center of much social life for my parents. My impression is that, maybe unusually for a country club, money didn't play a significant role. It was more friends who liked to socialize and enjoyed each other's company."

This log house already stood on the additional acreage that the club purchased in 1947, and helped introduce the idea of Keswick Estates, which more fully developed many decades later. (Photo courtesy of Kim Gibbs.)

"No Boots," Hurricane Hazel, and *Giant*

Drama in the little town of Keswick was very real in the 1950s. In January 1953 a tragedy occurred off Black Cat Road near the present east gate of the property. A United States Air Force B-26 aircraft carrying a pilot, a flight mechanic, and a passenger encountered unexpected freezing weather conditions while en route from Washington D.C. to Tucson, Arizona. The captain's last cry for help came thirty-three minutes after take-off, and the airplane dove at a near-vertical angle into a wooded portion of club property. Neighbors who came to the scene immediately after impact observed the smoldering wreckage as well as large ice shards on the ground – evidence of ice build-up on the airplane's wings, which were not equipped with rubberized boots allowing them to de-ice. The loss of three lives at once marks this event as the most deadly in the club's history.

Hurricane Hazel in October 1954 was another dramatic event, and Elisabeth Aaron, who lived in the log house near the east gate, recalled her mother speaking about it. "Communications and weather forecasting being what they were then, no one in the area expected the hurricane to retain such ferocious strength so far from its landfall in North Carolina. My mother said that the winds were deafening, so much so that a very large tree in the front of our house was upright one minute and down the next, and she didn't hear a thing. The eye passed directly over the house. It was still and serene in the eye, with blue sky above, but then the eye passed over and the winds resumed their incredible fury. My father was away for the day on business, and it took him hours of frantic driving to find passable roads to get back home. People were cleaning up for days, and we had to stay somewhere else for a while because without electricity we had no water. The house suffered no damage."

But not all drama is tragic or ferocious. In 1955 club members and local residents got rare glimpses of Hollywood stars. Scenes from the motion picture *Giant*, which starred Elizabeth Taylor and Rock Hudson, were shot on a local Keswick estate called Belmont as well as the new Keswick depot, which was built just after World War II and served the community until 1967. The movie was a magnet for publicity at a time when security concerns did not restrict visitors on film sets. Elisabeth Aaron recalled that the filming "was definitely quite a local happening…. My

Elizabeth Taylor and Rock Hudson are shown here on the set of the motion picture Giant, *filmed at the Keswick depot in 1955 with local residents milling on the set. (Photo courtesy of Ed Roseberry.)*

Keswick Airplane Crash (1953)

United States Air Force Captain Charles Stewart Herring, age 32, probably never heard of Keswick Country Club, and nothing suggested that the impending tragedy, soon to connect himself and two other men with the property, could be anything other than accidental. The official Air Force report, initially restricted and later released, provided the following details.

On Sunday, January 11th, 1953, Herring reported for duty at Bolling Air Force Base in Washington, DC. With 3453 hours of flying time under his belt, he was well qualified to pilot the B-26 aircraft on a proficiency flight to Tucson, Arizona, by way of Hensley Naval Air Station in Dallas, Texas. Air Force Staff Sargent James Russell Quaintance, age 23, also checked in that Sunday morning, to serve on board as flight mechanic, as did Michael C. Jenkins, age 55, a civilian who worked for the Department of the Navy, on board as a passenger. Equipment, conditions, and weather all seemed fine.

Captain Herring departed at 10:43 a.m. Ground temperature at take-off was 39 degrees. Captain Herring radioed at 11:10 a.m. that he was five minutes north of Gordonsville at 8000 feet, requesting permission to climb to 10,000 feet because of freezing rain. He was immediately cleared. At 11:11 a.m. he reported leaving 8000 feet. Richmond Radio heard a call at 11:14 a.m. on 135.9 megacycles: "Out of control – crashing." Thirty-three minutes after take-off, AF 2705 dove into a wooded portion near the present east gate of the 547 acres of property belonging to Keswick Country Club. Evidence indicated that it struck the ground at a near vertical angle.

Another pilot also departed Bolling AFB that morning with a similar flight plan, 20 minutes after Captain Herring. Before take-off, both captains had looked at wind charts and the latest weather map, and were aware that light rime icing had been indicated at 6000 feet for a short period of the flight. Rime ice is formed when high wind velocity combines with freezing air temperatures in freezing fog conditions; water droplets adhere in frozen state onto outer surfaces of objects such as the leading surfaces of aircraft flying through super-cold clouds. No one had thought it necessary to change their flight plans, including the Weather Officer who told them that by the time they got to Roanoke, "it would be CAVU all the way from there in" (CAVU meaning "Ceiling And Visibility Unlimited").

Charles Wesley Rice, who lived on Black Cat Road about 300 feet from the crash site and was in his kitchen when the accident occurred, stated in the report, "I heard the motors going and then they suddenly stopped.... I ran over to the scene... the gas smell was terrific.... I was the first person to arrive at the scene and I was joined by Mr. Fleming Hawley a few seconds later. I circled around for anyone who might have been alive or thrown clear. Some other man I don't know came around and wanted to start moving the plane to look for people inside. I told him it was no use." Mr. Rice's assessment was correct; there were no survivors. The report states simply: "aircraft completely demolished."

The second plane to leave Bolling that morning on that route was a B-25 and also encountered icy conditions. During the official investigation into the crash by the Aircraft Accident Board on January 19, 1953, the B-25's pilot, Captain Ewell D. Jacobs, stated that "Between Remington and Gordonsville the ice started to build up rather severely.... We used boots approximately every 4 to 5 minutes to clear the wings and tail." De-icing boots were thick rubber membranes installed over the leading surfaces of an airplane which could be inflated with compressed air to crack any ice that might have accumulated; subsequent airflow blew the ice away. Captain Jacobs estimated that by the time he reached Knoxville, 6 to 7 inches of rime ice had built up on the parts of his airplane that were not equipped with boots.

Evidently, the leading surfaces of Captain Herring's B-26, unfortunately equipped with no boots at all, also accumulated ice. Numerous witnesses found large shards scattered about the scene of the Keswick crash, including Virginia State Police Officer Douglas D. Hudson, who received a call at 11:18 a.m. These ice shards was likely the rime ice that cracked off the airplane's surfaces on impact. The Board's report found no violations and placed no blame for the tragic loss of three lives, but acknowledged that, "De-icers would probably have prevented this accident since the primary cause of the accident was ice."

The tragic loss of three lives marks this event among the most unfortunate in the property's history. The official report detailed material losses as well. Damage to Keswick Club property, besides the utter destruction of five to ten small pine trees, was minuscule: $150 reported. The total estimated monetary cost of the accident was $334,659, the aircraft alone being valued at $254,624. The wreckage covered an area approximately 75 yards in diameter, and a crater, about 10 feet deep and 25 feet across, remained after salvage work was completed. One small piece of the fuselage is said to have been secreted away to an undisclosed barn down the road, ever a reminder of the need for boots on January 11, 1953.

(Watermark image and crash details courtesy of Art Beltrone.)

mother had some choice recollections about Rock Hudson's presence in the area and said that Elizabeth's Taylor's violet eyes were remarkably beautiful, even more than film could capture."

Name Changes and the Back Nine

By the mid-1950s, various financial issues had resulted in changes of ownership. On June 30, 1955, the Keswick Cavalier Corporation, with Sidney Banks as its president, purchased 50.5% of the stock of the Keswick Corporation, which owned the buildings and land, and continued the operation. Banks changed the name of the club, as noted in letters extending "a cordial invitation to make application for membership" sent in early summer of 1955. These letters stated, "July 1st marks the opening date of the <u>NEW</u> Country Club of Keswick and the completion of many of the planned improvements. The improvement program for the season includes a complete revamping, renovation, and redecorating of the present swimming pool and cabanas (luncheon will be served at the pool and Cabana Club); construction of a new patio dance terrace adjacent to the pool and Cabana Club where dancing will be held each weekend through Labor Day; expansion and air-conditioning of the dining facilities; redecoration of the Grill; and reconditioning of the golf course to the greatest extent possible at this particular season of the year."

The member newsletter of that era, the *Keswick Club Crier*, announced in mid-summer of 1955 that "The opening of the club on July 9th wasn't the production we'd planned by a long shot – and the weatherman goofed completely." Nevertheless, "We've had compliments galore on the glamorizing [of the Pool

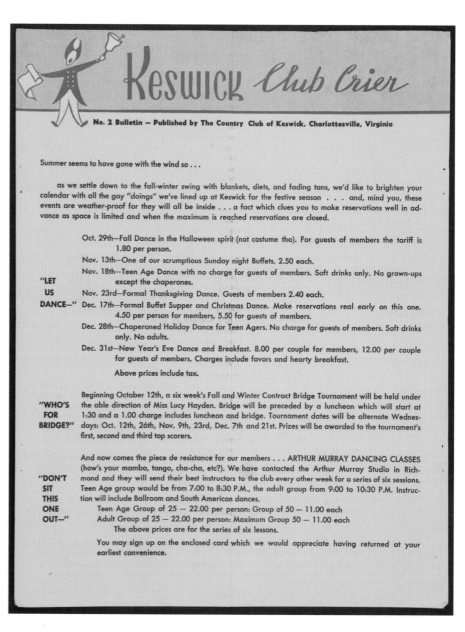

The Keswick Club Crier, *the club newsletter of the mid 1950s, gives a good idea of the variety of activities offered. (Image courtesy of UVa Special Collections.)*

and Cabana Club], ...dances will be held every Saturday evening...that is, rainless Saturday evenings.... [and] quite obviously with its new decor, the Grill is now the 'Hunt Room'... which is definitely horse crowd lingo." A *Club Crier* in the fall of 1955 announced Sunday night buffets for $2.50 each, Formal Buffet Supper and Christmas Dance for $4.50 per person for members ("Make reservations real early on this one"), and the New Year's Eve Dance and Breakfast for $8.00 per couple for members ("Charges include favors and hearty breakfast"). The club contracted with the Arthur Murray Dance Studio in Richmond, and arranged for dance instruction every other week at the club for a series of six sessions. Instruction included Ballroom and South American dances ("how's your mambo, tango, cha-cha, etc?").

Richard Slee became the new club manager in the summer of 1955 as well. His wife, Mary, joining him in October, combined her winning personality with her outstanding skills as master of the Buffet Supper, supervised all dining services, and offered home catering services for club members only. Donald Stevens had met the Slees in the Bahamas, where they managed another club. Dick Slee was a manager "par excellence," according to Helena (Nini) Sliney, daughter of Stevens. Also in 1955, Lou Shue became the new golf pro. "Speaking of golf," the newsletter continued, "we're all abeam with the turn-out of 72 golfers

A late 1950s brochure for the Country Club of Keswick contained fascinating elements. Note the reference to air conditioning (not to be taken for granted), the map that does not include Interstate Route 64 (the section heading west from Richmond did not open until 1971), the sketch of the front portico ("reflects the gracious charm synonymous with Charlottesville"), and the indication of "Cavalier" at Virginia Beach (site of a hotel operated by the same owners who took control of Keswick in 1955). (Image courtesy of Charlottesville Albemarle Historical Society.)

for the recent golf dinner." Golfers waiting for the second nine holes of the course received the news that "Work has started on the back nine and R. F. Loving and Fred Findlay, golf architects, are submitting their ideas on the completion of the golf course." A letter sent to a prospective member on September 17, 1955, stated, "Extensive work is still underway on the 'back nine' holes of the golf course and should be in excellent play condition by Spring [of 1956]."

A promotional brochure from the late 1950s describes the property as "A Private Country Club with the facilities of a resort hotel ... and a setting beautiful beyond compare in the rolling Blue Ridge foothills of Virginia's most traditional countryside. Here, on a 435 acre estate is an 18-hole championship golf course designed by Fred Findlay, Olympic size swimming pool with Cabana Club and terrace for sunning, lunching and evening dancing. The Tennis Club and Hunt Club stables further diversify the activities members and their guests enjoy. The main clubhouse with its attractive guest accommodations, dining room, ball room and Hunt Room is entirely air-conditioned and reflects the gracious charm synonymous with Charlottesville." The club's Schedule of Activities for March to September 1958 lists a Saturday evening Easter Buffet followed by dancing till 12:30 a.m., a Children's Easter Egg Hunt (3 p.m., no charge, bring your own basket), many golf luncheons, ladies day luncheons, game nights, and buffet suppers throughout the summer, and lots of dancing, including a formal spring dance on April 19.

Brochures and schedules of activities aside, the mid-1950s to mid-1960s were times of various internal dramas which led to further changes in leadership and ownership. Sidney Banks stepped out of the picture when his hotel group restructured, opening the door for Al Suttle, a successful businessman who owned a Chevrolet dealership in Petersburg and was chairman of the Richmond-Petersburg Turnpike Authority. An article about Suttle in the *Richmond News Leader* on March 4, 1957, highlighted his interest in skeet shooting, and stated that he "refuses to spend too much time behind the office desk." Suttle's Mecklenburg Development Corporation had been affiliated with the Jefferson Cavalier Corporation, which had held the reins of the club since 1955. Suttle bid $160,000 on the property at auction

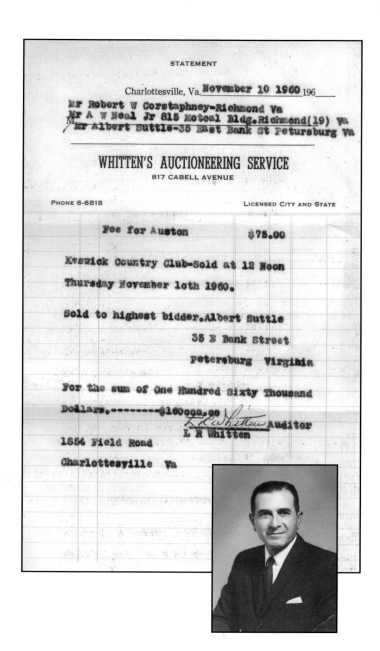

Mr. Albert Suttle placed the winning bid of $160,000 on the Country Club of Keswick in 1960, as seen in this auction receipt. The transaction reflects the pattern of changing ownership during this period. (Images courtesy of Al Suttle, Jr.)

on November 10, 1960, at which time, according to an article in the *Charlottesville Daily Progress* on November 11, 1960, the Country Club of Keswick had about 275 members. The auction took place on the front porch of the clubhouse. Suttle won the bid, assumed the title, and kept the Country Club of Keswick operating until 1964, when it would again change hands. In the meantime, the vision that Donald Stevens had had for this Keswick property at the beginning remained: it was, simply, "a place for people to have a good time."

Adorable children sit on the Villa staircase during the wedding of Charlie & Dot Kirtley in 1960; (left to right) Mark Wilson, Sarah Rennolds, Anne Rennolds, Debbie Rennolds, Beau Wilson. (Photo courtesy of Elizabeth Wilson.)

Chapter Three

A Real Family Club

The idea of a country club – a place with an established clubhouse for a specific set of members to come together for organized social and athletic activities – did not greatly catch on until well into the 20th century. Prohibition in the 1920s, the Depression in the 1930s, and the Second World War until 1945 kept the development of country clubs somewhat limited. When Villa Crawford was a fairly new structure on the Virginia landscape, people still entertained in their homes far more often than they gathered at a facility held in common through membership. But as communities recovered after the war and the future looked happier, and as music, film and technology began to take on entirely new forms, ideas about country club membership changed too.

More and more, people liked to meet at a place where they could eat, play, and enjoy each other's company in the leisure hours. They brought their children, their golf clubs, their tennis rackets, and their swimming suits. Some brought gin, vodka or other favorite drinks.

Unpretentious in its grandeur and centrally located yet almost inconspicuous, one particular cedar tree (to the far left in the photo) stands clearly visible in numerous archival photos, and stands to this day about 100 feet toward the mountain range from the original front door of Villa Crawford. Captured here on Polaroid presiding over an impressive ice skating rink in 1967, this same tree stood watch over the Crawford boys' miniature donkeys in 1914, over the comings and goings of more than a dozen owners and innumerable club members and hotel guests, over the swim ballet of 1951 and many weddings, receptions and dances, and over slowly maturing boxwoods, mostly now gone. The tree has lost strong limbs to lightning, and has doggedly survived hurricane-force winds, heavy snow, induced erosion, and the bulldozers of massive reconstruction projects. Yet it continues to do only what it has done for so long – majestically preside over the heart of the property. Like Villa Crawford itself, no matter what comes and goes, it stands tall. (Photo courtesy of Bob Reid.)

On a regular basis they attended luncheons, fashion shows, and buffet suppers; they took swim lessons, dance lessons, tennis lessons. They played in tournaments, hoped for trophies, and cheered for their friends. Country clubs became a new and dynamic kind of community space, and the Keswick Club of Virginia, as it came to be called in 1965, was no exception. Changing social norms, including this general gravitation toward country club membership, combined with a persistent optimism and strong leadership to set the stage for this very active period.

Between the changes of ownership and various behind-the-scenes corporation name changes, the puzzle of who owned the club, who was running it, and who had defaulted on it throughout the late 1950s and early 1960s became hard to follow, and some members became convinced that the situation was hopeless. Numbers went up and down – 350 resident members on opening day in 1948, increased by a hundred within a year, and reduced to 275 total members by 1960 and to a low of 55 in 1965. Local historian Barclay Rives commented that this property "rose and fell more times than ancient Troy." Some say it hung on by a thread, but it hung on. Bob and Elizabeth Wilson had moved to town in 1954 to open the Little Keswick School, which is still just down the road. They have fond memories of their first decade in Keswick, including the swimming pool on the club property during the early 1960s. Mrs. Wilson recalls, "We went over there all the time. We did not have a pool at the school, so we brought the children over there to swim – we had maybe 10 boys." Sandra (Brown) Burke, who had been a teenage participant in the 1951 swim ballet, brought her own children during this time as well. They were among a good number of residents who continued to use and enjoy the pool, tennis courts and golf course despite varying levels of solvency and multiple name changes. In 1964 the Country Club of Keswick had become the Albemarle Country Club, which in 1965 became the University Club, and later that year became the Keswick

July, 1965: Susan Wilson Lyons enjoying the club's pool with Marc Columbus, who went on to become headmaster of Little Keswick School. (Photo courtesy of Elizabeth Wilson.)

This aerial photograph, taken in May of 1964, shows a good deal of the golf course, the C&O railroad line criss-crossing Keswick Road, and the "new" Keswick depot in the bottom right hand corner. Hunt Club Drive, the main entrance onto the grounds off of Route 22, would be off to the bottom right, but is not visible in this image. (Photo by Ed Roseberry.)

Club of Virginia. Prospective owners with ambition continued to be attracted to the property.

One owner in particular made a significant impact on the club. From 1965 until 1971, Knox Turnbull was arguably the force behind its renewed energy, increased membership, and ambitious direction. John L. Snook, a University of Virginia professor at that time and a member of the club's board of directors in 1970 and 1971, called him "a brilliant and courageous businessman" in an article summarizing the club's history, published in the *Daily Progress* on August 7, 1983. Turnbull had earned his law degree at the University of Virginia in 1941 and served in the U.S. Navy during the entire period of World War II. He returned to Charlottesville after the war and began a successful career in the insurance business. By 1950 he was heading a permanent fundraising organization for the University called "Mr. Jefferson's Sponsors," and in 1960 was a committeeman for Virginians for Conservative Political Action, speaking publicly for school integration. In 1962 Turnbull became a visiting professor of law at the University, while keeping his hand in numerous business endeavors, including the Keswick Club of Virginia.

Knox Turnbull, shown in 1961, promoted more activities, many capital improvements, and new membership criteria during his tenure. His determination and leadership increased membership from a low of 55 in 1965 to a high of 808 at the time of his death in 1971.

Turnbull was determined to make the Keswick Club of Virginia the best club anywhere, and he left lasting impressions. Bob Reid, tennis pro while Turnbull held the reins, said, "He was able to take it over. His idea was to orient it toward the university, and for eight years it was a very delightful place to go – an all-service club with golf course, tennis courts, pool, everything. It was a wonderful club." Snook put it this way: "It was a real family club. You could go out there on a Saturday, take your clubs, your swimming trunks, tennis racket and half a gallon of vodka and have a great time." Club President Warren C. Judge, Jr. stated in the club newsletter in June of 1971 that "no Club within 500 miles can offer such wide-range, year-round recreational facilities." Mike Miller, who became the club's golf pro in the late 1970s (after the Turnbull period), recalled, "I always heard great things about Knox. People would come up to me and say, 'Boy, you should have seen this place *then*.'"

Under Turnbull's leadership, the Keswick Club of Virginia changed in various ways: more activities, many capital improvements, and new membership criteria. The club became much more of a year-

New wall-to-wall carpeting in the Hunt Room in 1970 was just one of many capital improvements made on the property while it was called the Keswick Club of Virginia. (Photo courtesy of Cindy (Sowers) Barnes.)

It was a great honor for Reverend Henry Mitchell and his wife Gertrude to be platform guests at the Bicentennial (1976) Naturalization Ceremony at Monticello at which then-President Gerald R. Ford spoke. Rev. and Mrs. Mitchell and their family, on the invitation of Knox Turnbull in 1965, were the first members to redefine the club's former policy. No longer was the Keswick Club, as described in a letter to potential members in 1955, an "organization for members and their guests who are congenial and of similar backgrounds and tastes." (Photo courtesy of Gerald R. Ford Library.)

round center of activity. There was so much to do that a single-spaced, three-page newsletter was printed monthly to help members keep track of the numerous and various tournaments and social events. Dottie Reynolds, whose husband became the club's golf pro in 1966, recalls the monthly formal dinner dances with tuxedos required, the Friday Night Scotch Foursomes, and costume balls. She said, "The year the contraceptive pill was introduced, we had one couple who came as the Pope and the Pill. They won of course!"

Under Turnbull's direction, club facilities also improved greatly and gained many exciting features for family fun. Capital improvements included an outdoor ice rink; a rope tow for skiing; seven additional tennis courts, totaling ten, with a heated, lighted bubble over three of them; and a new Olympic-size pool with its own space bubble, just north of the oval pool (both since removed). The oval, steel swimming pool was repainted and refurbished, with new lights installed; the golf locker rooms were completely redecorated with new wall-to-wall carpeting; new oriental rugs were purchased for the main rooms and new wall-to-wall carpeting for Hunt Room; and all windows were completely insulated.

Knox Turnbull also invited Dick and Mary Slee, who had run the club for two years in the 1950s, to return in 1965. Their daughter, Debbie Gibbs, recalls, "[Turnbull] called my father because he had been successful in the Bahamas in getting clubs to open their doors to different races." Among his other goals, Turnbull was determined to change the membership criteria that had been firmly in place up until then, a move which took "a great deal of courage," according to Barclay Rives. That same year, Reverend Henry Mitchell, rector of the Trinity Episcopal Church in Charlottesville, and his wife Gertrude and their two children were invited to become club members. "The Mitchell's were lovely, lovely people," said Mrs. Gibbs.

Dick and Mary Slee continued for the next two years to do what they did best. Mrs. Gibbs said, "My mother and dad really knew how to run a club. My mother took care of the food – people would come out just for that. She just kept things going – had fashion shows, fondue nights – people would come out on Sunday nights and sit by the fire and have fondue." Bob Reid said, "Mary Slee was not a country person, but rather a big city type who dressed the part, and a whiz in the kitchen." Dick and Mary Slee and their son Prescott lived on the second floor of the clubhouse; Room 9 was used as their living room. Their daughter shared the third floor with a girlfriend who was the club's lifeguard. Prescott's poodle "De De" made a habit of greeting people from the top of the stairs.

On her wedding day at the Keswick Club on February 17, 1967, Debbie Gibbs posed with her parents, club managers Richard & Mary Slee. Debbie and Randy's bridal party gathered in what is now the snooker room. (Photos courtesy of Debbie Gibbs.)

Wintertime Fun

In 1967 Knox Turnbull had an outdoor ice rink installed on the expanded swimming pool patio that had been laid in 1955 (in warmer weather this patio was also the outdoor dance floor). Club members bundled up on the days that were cold enough and skated to their heart's content. Guests of members did not even need to be accompanied by the member in order to take advantage of the ice. In its second season, 1967-68, the rink maintained almost continuous operation from mid-November onward; its schedule was posted in the "Rink Office," as well as outside. The Teenage Rink Party on January 19, 1968, included a "bonfire and wiener roast," and cost $1.50 per person including "warming room refreshments," skating fee, and rental skates. The Single Member's Party a week later began at the Ice Rink at 7:00 p.m. However, as the January 1968 newsletter stated, "Anyone not wishing to skate may go directly to the 19th Hole, but 'Do not pass Go, Do not collect $200.00!' Rental skates and use of the ice rink – $1.00 per person. B.Y.O.L." (Bring[ing] Your Own Liquor was the norm during this time.) The February 1971 newsletter reported that about 600 people had used the rink during the first month of its operation that winter.

Skating was not the only outdoor wintertime activity for adults and children. As a rule, Virginia does not get the same snowfall as states to the north and west, but evidently there was enough of a track record and plenty of hope for it in the late 60s. The club newsletter of January 1968 claimed that "Keswick's ski slope is in much better condition this year. The new positioning of the rope tow will give better access to both sides of the slope, hay has been spread to protect the tow track and release areas, the bank of the upper tee has been angled to permit easier climbing with skis on, and the entire slope area is now well lighted for late afternoon and evening skiing. All we need now is snow!"

Club members throughout the 1960s had good reason to hope for plenty of snow to make for great outdoor winter activities. In 1961 the Stevens children and their dog enjoyed tobogganing down the hill that sloped away from the oval pool – notice the brick uprights that surrounded the pool. During 1966-67, the first season that the club had an ice rink, members and guests such as these three "skating friends" paid $1.00 per person to rent skates and enjoy the ice. Above, a rope tow made skiing possible. (Sledding photo courtesy of Rosely Stevens; skating photo courtesy of Bob Reid.)

"The Steel Pool...Beautiful, Man!"

During the long, warm summer that is typical of Virginia, Keswick Club members made good use of the oval, steel pool that had been a favorite recreational spot since 1948. It now became a place of instruction as well. The member newsletter of May 1967 stated: "Both group and private lessons will be offered. Lesson fees: Private – $4.00 per half hour, $6.00 per hour. Group – minimum of 10 lesson series at $1.00 per lesson (one hour long) per child. Class size will be 5 minimum to 10 maximum but there will be enough instructors to run several classes concurrently."

On the recreational side, good, clean fun turned so muddy one year, "you could almost walk across that pool," said Don Celec, bartender at the time, who remembers one prank very well. John Ney had replaced Richard Slee as general manager in January of 1968 when the Slees chose to return to the Bahamas, and one challenge of Ney's first year happened on a major holiday, the 4th of July. Celec related, "The staff came that morning to get everything ready and found that the pool had been drained. Turned out Gordon Stevens and Jimmy New had opened the valve and let all the water out – it had drained all the way to the pond. Well, you can't have the 4th of July without a pool, so they called in an emergency crew to pump the water back. They got everything all set up, then went off to get something to eat. What they didn't know was that the float dropped to the bottom of the pond and started sucking silt and mud up into the pool. There were snakes and frogs and everything in there. I made a sign that said 'Pool Closed,' and it took them two weeks to get that mess cleaned up."

Interest in swimming was in no way dampened by two weeks without a pool, and with membership rolls growing along with interest in competitive swimming, another pool was soon in the plans. In 1969 a 25-meter, five-lane pool opened, greatly increasing options for private and group swim lessons available to club members of all ages, as well as adult-only swimming and life saving courses. When membership and interest continued to grow, summer-only swimming proved to be a limitation, and a heated space bubble was erected over the Olympic-length pool with heaters for both the air and the water, again greatly increasing options.

Alice Matthews set up a "Swim and Slim" club: "Come on, girls!" encouraged the March 1971 newsletter. "You have wanted this for a couple of years. Now we have the warm bubble and an expert leader. You don't have to swim, but you will limber up and get in shape for Spring!

As seen in this aerial view, the second pool, installed in 1969, was located just north (to the right) of the oval pool; a space bubble was installed over it to allow for winter swimming. The second story of the cabanas had been were removed by this time. Note the club's restaurant, the "Hunt Room," on the main level facing the golf course, quite similar to how Fossett's is oriented in the hotel now, as well as the golf shop extending on the lower left. The roof of the golf shop was used as a terrace; the white objects on it are actually umbrellas over tables (the event on page 65, lower left-hand image, takes place on this terrace). Also note the patio just south (to the left) of the oval pool, used for summertime "tea dances" on Sunday afternoons and the ice rink in the winter. Both pools were removed during later renovations and in 2003 the horizon pool replaced the circular driveway north of the front portico. The main section of the original Villa Crawford, with its double chimneys on the far side, the three gables above the northern portico, and the single chimney on the near side, and the large cedar tree (to the left of the oval pool and to the right of the horizon pool) are among the only elements seen in both images. (Photo courtesy of Bob Paxton; inset courtesy of Orient-Express Image Library.)

The program will be more fun if we have more participants for then you won't feel alone if Alice goes a bit fast and you want to sit one out. Put on some old slacks, bring a beach towel and come join the fun." Coached by Mrs. James Garrison, the water ballet program picked up where the "Aqua Maids" of 1951 had left off, and performed shows of their own. Dottie Reynolds remembers one set to "New York, New York." She said, "I can probably keep from drowning, but I am not a wonderful swimmer. The show was synchronized to music, and the pool wasn't so deep, so it looked really pretty. We laughed our heads off during rehearsals, but we were very good for the performance."

Additionally, "All interested boys and girls" were urged to participate on the swim team. The "Marlins" were divided into three groups – 12-and-older, 11-and-under, and anyone who could swim the length of the pool. The "entire swimming operation" was managed initially by Bud Beardmore, as announced in the May 1968 newsletter, and later by Ralph Law, who led the team to a great record in 1971. The fee for a "swimming team" member was $8.00 per month.

Without the space bubble (and the support of the membership and the board of directors behind it), such programs would not have been as extensive. Though some did question the capital expenditure, a sense of pride and confidence grew and grew as the Keswick swimmers were able to hold winter meets, for example, with the University of Virginia pool team, combining similar ages and abilities, then redividing the swimmers to balance

The oval, steel pool was always a popular place for club members and their guests to cool off on hot Virginia summer days. (Late 1960s photo courtesy of Harriet and Dan Mohler.)

KESWICK CLUB OF VIRGINIA NEWSLETTER

VOL. V, NO. 8   KESWICK, VIRGINIA   AUGUST 1971

GOURMET DINNER SLATED FOR SATURDAY, AUGUST 7

THE PRESIDENT'S CORNER

Membership in the Keswick Club of Virginia has reached a grand total of 801. This consists of 601 Resident Members and exactly 200 Non-Resident Members.

We need 399 additional Resident Members to reach the Club's goal of 1000 Resident Members. When this figure is reached, each member will receive a Certificate of Membership. This can then be redeemed, when there is a waiting list, for the full amount paid as initiation fee, if the member wishes to resign for any reason or if he dies.

Present members who are leaving the area should consider the advisability of becoming Non-Resident Members. By so doing, they would become eligible to receive a Membership Certificate when the 1000 Resident Member goal is reached. Non-Resident Members, who have never been Resident Members, are not eligible to receive Membership Certificates.

The Keswick Club of Virginia is continuing to maintain its average of almost a new member a day. With the University opening in a few weeks, scores of new families are moving into the area.

As we all know, the fall is one of the most beautiful times at Keswick. Golf and tennis are at their peak; and this year, for the first time in the Charlottesville area, swimming will become a year-round activity. We will erect our swimming pool bubble in September and continue to swim throughout the winter. Our tennis bubble will go up in November.

Find a new member for your Club. One of our members remarked last week that he had gotten us his new member. Don't stop with one! Bring your friends into the Keswick Club. Give them an opportunity to enjoy the social contacts, the fun and our unequalled sports facilities.

Warren C. Judge, Jr.

Please Observe Speed Limit

Remember! The speed limit within the Keswick Club gates is 10 miles per hour—for cars, motorbikes, minibikes—all forms of transportation.

A gourmet treat is in store for Keswick members the night of Saturday, August 7th! Specially processed milk-fed veal, a delicacy in the finest restaurants in France, will be served five different ways. Most Americans have never tasted milk-fed veal which can be cut with a fork.

The story of how the Keswick Club of Virginia came by its milk-fed veal is an interesting one. Mr. Frank Walker, Jr., who operates the extremely modern Rosni Farms in Madison County (bordering Orange, Va.), is a pioneer in the United States in the use of the Maternal Robot.

The Maternal Robot is an automatic milk feeding machine designed to supplement Nature's way of suckling calves. It was invented by a French farmer six years ago. More than 8000 of the machines are in use in Europe but it has only recently been introduced into the United States. Hay is an unnecessary supplement when calves are raised on the automatic feeder. The feeder operates 24 hours enabling the calf to have a "snack" at any time. The net result is a superior, prime quality veal obtainable only in the most expensive restaurants in this country.

Our Chef, James Turner, and new Assistant Chef, John Cheek, have visited Mr. Walker's Holstein Dairy and Breeding Farm and on the same trip called on the processor to tell him how they wanted the veal dressed out.

At this special dinner, the Club will serve veal as follows:

    Crown Roast
    Stuffed Breast of Veal
    Veal Scallopini
    Cuscinetti di Vitello
    Veal Cutlets

The entire dinner will be sumptuous, topped off with strawberry shortcake. The price is $6.55 per person, considerably less than famed restaurants charge for veal that would not be of the superior, prime quality of Rosni Farms veal.

Make your reservations now for a dinner that you will not forget. Maternal Robot has requested permission to invite 25 Government and State officials to the Keswick Club's "veal deal." We will serve 180 pounds of Virginia style, European milk-fed veal with a little French cuisine thrown in for good measure. The time: 7 to 9 p.m., Saturday, August 7.

Symbols of an era: Embroidered patches like this were sewn onto men's blazers during this time, giving them a distinguished and uniform look. A sample newsletter shows the look that prevailed from May 1967 through July 1972. (Patch courtesy of Dottie Reynolds; newsletter courtesy of George Reynolds.)

the skills for the races. Competing in the winter also gave the Marlins a competitive edge in the summer. The May 1971 newsletter stated that "the Swimming Bubble will remain up until about May 15 as Ralph Law continues to ready his teams for the outdoor season. Our Marlins should be tough competition for anyone this summer." The August newsletter boasted that the team performed so well that they defeated even the Fairview Swim Club, a "milestone in the history of the Jefferson Swim League" because Fairview had been undefeated in previous years.

Between the ice rink and the indoor swimming pool, the Keswick Club implied in the February 1971 newsletter its intention to undo the impression that "at most clubs, teenagers are a problem.... We are offering our youngsters two of the healthiest, life-time, carry-over sports in the business. We expect more than 100 boys and girls to use the pool for swim team and swimming class instruction this winter."

The excitement about the indoor pool did not reduce enthusiasm for the outdoor pool, which was in fact enjoyed so much that it warranted a major overhaul in 1971. The maintenance team, headed by Bill Kirby, scraped at least six coats of paint off of the interior and repainted it "a beautiful birds-egg blue." New lights were also installed in time for the season's opening day on May 29. Thus the section heading from the June 1971 club newsletter: "The Steel Pool... Beautiful, Man!"

Golf at the Keswick Club: One "Swinging Season" After Another

Though Knox Turnbull was more enthusiastic about tennis than about golf, the activities were equally popular. Initially, however, there was a lot of work to do on the golf course. Bobby Bowers remembers the first time he saw it with PGA golf professional Glenn Reynolds, in March of 1966. "Glenn and I rode a cart around the course to look it over. The greens were in bad shape, many being overrun with crabgrass. The fairways, while green, had lots of growth that was foreign to good fairways. Glenn said, 'We're going to turn this place into a showcase.'" And that he did. Reynolds' team included Louis Moore, honored in 1972 for one quarter century of golf course maintenance at Keswick, which he began with Fred Findlay's course in 1947, and Neal Harless, the greenskeeper at Galax Country Club who was hired to come help. The club newsletter of May 1968 suggested that the success of the Dogwood Festival Pro-Am Tournament, held in April, was "due in large measure to the condition of the course. Many of the pros maintained that the layout was in the finest shape ever. Accolades go to head pro, Glenn Reynolds, and his crew, who worked long hours to get the course in such good shape." Members and guests enjoyed numerous events and tournaments, including the Keswick Golf Team playing the University of Virginia team for fun and practice; the annual Dogwood Festival Tournaments (the 18th Annual in 1967); the Jefferson Cup Tournament, an invitational begun in 1967 that drew many members of the community at large; and the Winter Dog Fight Tournaments.

Glenn Reynolds was also instrumental in expanding the women's golf program by

Glenn Reynolds was the head golf professional at the Keswick Club from 1966-72. (Photo courtesy of Dottie Reynolds.)

Louis Moore was honored in the June 1972 club newsletter for his 25 years of dedicated service keeping the greens in excellent condition.

"I will always remember the fantastic view looking back up to the very stately clubhouse," said Richard Leake, who played in many tournaments. These photographs show the back of the clubhouse from two different angles: above, seen from the 9th hole on the par 73 course, and below, with a 1968 Oldsmobile Cutlass convertible embellished for the Dogwood Festival. Directly above the cart barn was the Hunt Room, one of the club's two dining rooms. (Top photo courtesy of Dottie Reynolds; bottom photo courtesy of Ed Roseberry.)

On the weekend of August 3-4, 1968, the Keswick Club sponsored the second annual Jefferson Cup Golf Tournament. Ed Roseberry's photos give an overview of the social scenes, the winners, and the fashions of the time.

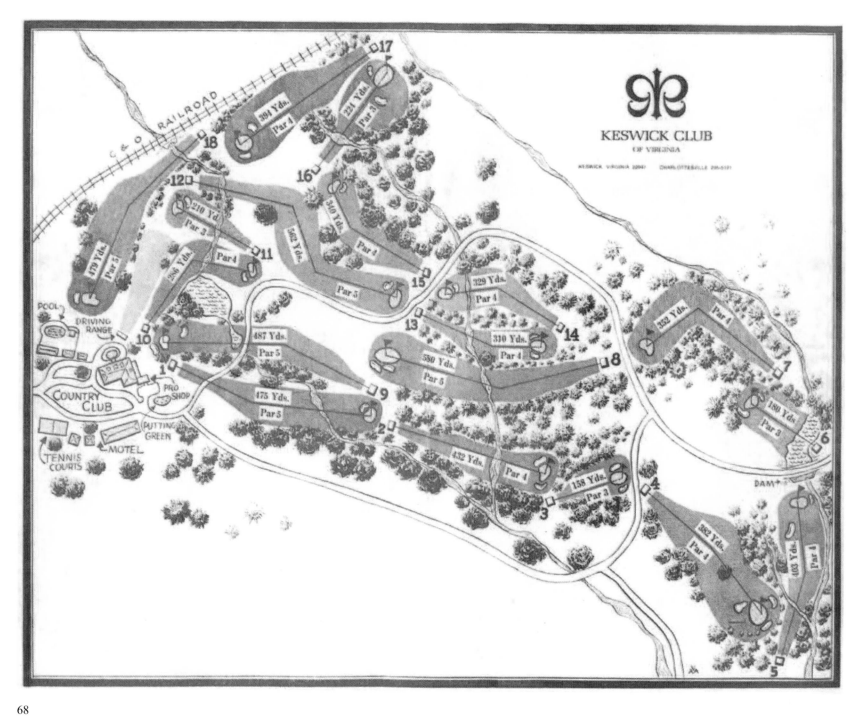

KESWICK CLUB
OF VIRGINIA

KESWICK, VIRGINIA 22947   CHARLOTTESVILLE 295-6121

C & O RAILROAD

394 Yds.
Par 4

224 Yds.
Par 3

17

18

12

210 Yd.
Par 3

479 Yds.
Par 5

256 Yds.

11

Par 4

562 Yds.

340 Yds.
Par 4

16

15

Par 5

13

329 Yds.
Par 4

310 Yds.
Par 4

14

8

352 Yds.

Par 4

7

POOL

DRIVING
RANGE

10

487 Yds.
Par 5

580 Yds.
Par 5

9

180 Yds.
Par 3

6

COUNTRY
CLUB

PRO
SHOP

1

475 Yds.
Par 5

2

432 Yds.
Par 4

158 Yds.
Par 3

4

DAM

PUTTING
GREEN

MOTEL

TENNIS
COURTS

3

352 Yds.
Par 4

403 Yds.
Par 4

5

68

wholeheartedly supporting the Ladies Golf Association, providing instructional clinics, and helping to arrange special events. The March 1971 club newsletter relates that "The Ladies Golf Association will hold their annual spring luncheon meeting March 16 at 12:30 in the Hunt Room. Make your reservations at the Club early. Luncheon is $2.50, including tax and tip. Weather permitting, our regular Tuesday play will start Tuesday March 23 at 9:00 a.m. We are planning a swinging season and even if you have never joined us before, come on out and share the fun."

By far the golf events that got the most press were the back-to-back State Open tournaments, held in both 1969 and 1970. The challenging 6583-yard par 73 Keswick course, said the description in the 42nd Annual Virginia State Open Golf Championship program, was "very scenic and offers a wide variety of golf course situations. The front nine holes are predominantly wooded, and the back nine are almost all open. There is an abundance of streams which add to the beauty of the course as well as provide natural hazards." In 1969 Herb Hooper and Chandler Harper were among those professionals playing for the $6000 total purse, of which the professional winner's take was $4775 and the amateur's was $200.

The original layout of the golf course is seen in this widely used map (left), and a point of interest (above) to those who may recall the original Villa Crawford, constructed in 1912, and its 100 white marble columns forming a peristyle on the east lawn (visible in the black and white photo on page 10, far left): In 1969 one of those marble columns still stood where these golfers waited their turn on the 10th tee. Also see page 66, upper left-hand photo and page 67, upper-right. No other evidence of these columns remains. (Color photo courtesy of Dottie Reynolds; black & white photo courtesy of K. Edward Lay, UVa Special Collections.)

The Keswick Club Racqueteers

The ten tennis courts – three more had been opened for play in the spring of 1967 – also saw a lot of activity. Lessons, clinics, round robins, and tournaments, all designed to generate interest in the game, kept pro Bob Reid very busy. Tennis ladders were another way to encourage players to get to know other players of similar skill level. Players signed up in the tennis shop, located in the first small building on the right near the west entrance (now the sales office), and results of who won the match helped determine who played whom in subsequent matches. The club newsletter encouraged the ladders: "This sort of play is great for your game and helps to make all of the Keswick Club racqueteers better acquainted." The newsletter of May 1968 also promoted the Ladies Day clinics that were to be held every Tuesday in May. Bob Reid would be conducting "supervised play, including instructional assistance in stroke technique and court tactics. There will be a charge of $1.00 per person per session. Make this a regular thing and stay over for the buffet luncheon in the Hunt Room – remember, tennis attire is acceptable!" In the tennis shop, ladies could find "a wonderful selection of the latest tennis dresses."

In the spring of 1968, noted player Alphonso Smith, honored in 1967 for his service to senior tennis by the USTA Seniors'

This 1968 tennis event at the club shows spectators seated in front of the concession stand waiting for the match to begin. The stand has been moved closer to the west gate and now serves as a flower shed. The building directly behind the concession stand was the tennis shop and office. It has not been moved, but is now the sales office. (Photo courtesy of Bob Reid.) Above, the Keswick Club tennis bubble, as seen in a club pamphlet of the time.

Experience Abounds

Progress Photo By John Atkins

Bob Reid (kneeling) with 54 years of playing tennis joins C. Alphonso (standing left) with 58 years, Donn Bent with 62 years and Eddie von Selzam and his 70 years of experience to put 264 years of playing tennis on one court. All four have held or currently hold state, regional or national rankings. Their experience grows daily as they continue to participate actively in tennis activities.

Tennis was very popular at the Keswick Club. Bob Reid, tennis pro, is shown in this photograph with Alphonso Smith, Donn Bent, and Eddie von Selzam. Mr. Reid at age 96 shared his many memories. When asked during the interview about the tennis whites that the players in the photograph are wearing, Mr. Reid unhesitatingly responded, "You know, I watch those guys on TV now, and I just don't understand how those long baggy shorts can be comfortable!" (Charlottesville Daily Progress photo by John Atkins.)

Committee, came to the club to do research for an article he was writing about tennis at Keswick for *World Tennis* magazine. Turnbull convinced "Smithy," as he was called, to return to Keswick and work with Bob Reid to further strengthen the program. Smith's clout helped bring exhibition matches to the Keswick Club featuring top players of the day. Club members remember Billy Jean King coming, as well as when Arthur Ashe played an exhibition match against Charlie Pasarell on November 2, 1969. Arthur Ashe won the first U.S. Open Tennis Championship at Forest Hills in 1968, and in 1975 became the first African American to win the men's singles title at Wimbledon. Cindy (Sowers) Barnes, whose father managed accounts for Knox Turnbull from a third-floor office, remembers when Lynda Bird Johnson, daughter of President Lyndon Baines Johnson, took tennis lessons wearing red tennis shoes. "Everything was white back then," she said, but "that's all she had." (Miss Johnson's fiance, Chuck Robb, who later became Governor of Virginia, received his law degree from the University of Virginia in 1973.) In September of 1971, the club sponsored the National 70 Clay Court Tennis Championships with players from at least eleven states and Canada entered. The official U.S. Lawn Tennis Association event was for players 70 or older, such as Walter Wesbrook, who had won the 1925 National Clay Court Doubles Championships with Harvey Snodgrass. The April newsletter noted that Cary Grant had been asked to play in the tournament with Jean Borotra, a tennis star of the 1920s, but no subsequent mention of this potentially crowd-drawing event led to the assumption that Mr. Grant had a scheduling conflict.

Bob Reid was proud to say that the tennis bubble, opened for the 1970-71 winter season, gave the Keswick Club of Virginia the distinction of having the first indoor courts south of Washington, D.C., and enthusiasm for it was huge; the February 1971 newsletter notes that "One obvious enthusiast has called the tennis bubble 'the most important event in Charlottesville since the passing of Thomas Jefferson.'" The March 1971 newsletter noted that "More and more tennis players are taking advantage of Keswick's fine indoor facility....

Weekday use has risen from an average in January of from 50-60% capacity to present utilization of about 80%. Week-end use averages close to 90%." The May 1971 newsletter reported that "Approximately 1500 players a month laughed at the cold, the snow, the rain, the wind to play, day and night, throughout the winter." Winter tennis included fun events such as the "Tennis-Golf Mixed Doubles Championships" also called a "Fiasco in the Tennis Bubble" in February 1971. "Each team consisted of a tennis player paired with a golfer. While the quality of the tennis is open to question, much fun was had by all. Beer and more solid refreshments were available and indulged in by the participants as the tennis showed. In the finals, Sally Sowers and Alfonso Smith eked out a 7-5 win over Ann Cohen and Bob Reid. Sally's gay bloomers were a deciding factor in her team's victory." Tennis players were subtly warned not to get too puffed up about their higher skill levels. To balance things out, "The tournament will be replayed on the golf course in the spring."

COMPARISON OF CLUB COSTS AND FACILITIES					
CLUB	Initiation Fee	Annual Dues All Privileges	Indoor Tennis Courts	Indoor Swimming	Ice Skating
Farmington C C	$1000	$500	No	No	No
Country Club of Virginia (Richmond)	$2000	$600	Yes	No	No
Army Navy C C Arlington, Va.	$2400	$480	No	No	No
Chevy Chase Club (Chevy Chase, Md.)	$4000	$750	No	No	No
Kenwood Golf & C C (Bethesda, Md.)	$1500	$456	No	No	No
Keswick Club of Va.	$500	$325	Yes	Yes	Yes

'The greatest little club in the USA': "Whatever we call it," stated Warren C. Judge, Jr., in the September 1971 club newsletter, "is not as important as our recognition that the Keswick Club is the best buy in clubs today, and that we have a great little thing going here in Jefferson's Country."

The Tennis-Golf Mixed Championships provided a humorous bone of contention, but tennis and swimming enthusiasts were apparently also somewhat at odds with the golfers in regard to the two space bubbles that were erected. In particular, "There seems to be a feeling that money intended for improvements to the golf course was diverted to tennis and swimming. This is not the case at all," stated club president Warren Judge in the February 1971 newsletter. Club owners and board members justified their decision with a thorough explanation of the "sharp let-down in business during the winter months, the same as practically all other clubs," and stated that being able to offer tennis and swimming in the winter "is increasing the pleasure of members and their families, ... helping to increase restaurant and bar business, ... and making the Club more attractive to potential members.... We can't put a bubble over the golf course but come March and golf architect Joe Finger's recommendations, we can look forward to improvements on the course. It is a simple fact we should face up to that the total amount spent for both the tennis and swimming pool bubbles would scarcely make a ripple on a few fairways. I am confident that golf will share in the over-all improvement program being implemented at Keswick." In the May 1972 newsletter, members were reminded that it cost in excess of $50,000 per year, labor and materials, to maintain the golf course, plus "a considerable amount of expertise." The war against weeds was constant, but "the Club spends a lot of gold and constantly works to make it turn out green."

In All Its Glory

The overall improvements at the Keswick Club led to the May 1971 newsletter headline: THE KESWICK CLUB IN ALL ITS GLORY. By June, membership had reached an all-time high of 761. By August, 801. The principle factors in this tremendous growth, according to Judge, were "greater use of Club facilities, economics in operation, more exact division of managerial responsibilities, and a new team spirit among our members." Judge compared the costs of membership at Keswick with that of comparable clubs and noted that Keswick's initiation fee was far below the average and half that of the other local club, that dues were considerably less, and that "No club in the area can approach Keswick's year-round sports facilities."

Unquestionably, the club had become what Donald Stevens had envisioned from the start: people were having a good time in many ways – playing bridge, going on a hayride, enjoying Alice MacInnis's Swim & Slim's, Mrs. Robertson's swim ballets and Neil Kittle's Shakespeare plays, joining the swim team, learning Japanese flower arranging, sprucing up the 19th Hole, tweaking their tennis stroke, attending book swapping parties, tuning up their golf swing, attending fashion shows, and eating cheese fondue... and oysters. Don't forget the oysters. Don't forget the food.

More than 100 people were turned away from the January 20, 1971, Oyster Buffet because they failed to make reservations. The "sumptuous Oyster Buffets" that served "oysters every way known to man – on the half shell, oyster stew, hot, cold, plain, and fancy (of course, sumpin' for the landlubbers)" were highly popular. And not only for dinner – Cindy (Sowers) Barnes and Pat (Spicer) Napoleon remember that as young teenagers they snuck into the kitchen and begged the cooks for oysters out of the can – their version of "on the half shell." Chef James Turner presented milk-fed veal in numerous forms later that year through a deal with Rosni Farms in Madison County, an operation that used a "Maternal Robot" to help feed the calves. The club hosted a gourmet dinner where the veal was served five delectable ways on August 7, 1971, plus strawberry shortcake, calling it a "veal

Waverly Jordan had trained under Chef Gaines in the late 1940s, and became Keswick Club's new chef in January of 1972.

deal" for $6.55 per person, and expected to serve "180 pounds of Virginia style, European milk-fed veal with a little French cuisine thrown in for good measure." Bob Reid always said they didn't charge enough for the food.

Labor Day weekend of 1971 was as active as any other. Club Championships were played on the golf course throughout the weekend, the National Clay Court Tennis Championships were held, a pool-side "dress as you wish" dance was held on Saturday, a swim meet was held on Monday, as well as the Labor Day picnic with hay rides "for the youngsters" in the afternoon and a "box lunch of fried chicken, cole slaw, potato salad, ice cream, soft drinks, etc. will be served at 6 p.m. Price $2.00."

On Tuesday, September 7, club members were shocked to learn that Knox Turnbull had died. Within the following year, despite numerous events still being held, plans still being made, and hopes continually being kindled, despite Eve Turnbull, Knox's widow, directing that the club continue as a monument to her husband, despite 808 members on Labor Day weekend, the situation changed dramatically at the Keswick Club of Virginia. Complications surfaced, disappointment and sadness permeated the ranks, and people began to float away.

Many reflected on what had made the club so special and successful, and almost unanimously credited Knox Turnbull. The October 1971 newsletter noted that "a dirty ashtray in the 19th Hole or a faulty gate latch concerned him as much as the balance sheet," and reminded members that even though membership had reached its all-time low (55 in 1965) when he first made the club completely non-discriminatory, he "never wavered." He was sure the Keswick Club could be the

Times were changing, and from the mid-1960s until the early-1970s, the Keswick Club was thriving. Janet Meade of Charlottesville and Mrs. Tucker Brown of Danville enjoyed a wedding reception in June of 1966 in what is now the library of Keswick Hall. Ms. Meade was the University of Virginia's first female Ph. D. recipient. Ed Roseberry won an award for this photograph in 1967 in an Eastman Kodak national competition. (Photo courtesy of Ed Roseberry.)

kind of place where people would marvel at their ability to look past individual differences *and* have fun together. Dan Mohler and Paul Gaston were both professors at the University of Virginia at the time, and both affirmed that the Keswick Club's membership criteria gave more people a reason to come. Gaston, author of *Coming of Age in Utopia: The Odyssey of an Idea*, recalls playing tennis many times at the club, and many times under the bubble. He decided to join in the mid-1960s after some of his colleagues told him what was going on. His wife had questioned him because they were "not country club people," but Gaston told her, "Knox Turnbull is going to have the first integrated club in Virginia, and it is the duty of all good liberals to go out and join." Support for the idea was not immediate, nor universal. Bob Reid said, "Charlottesville wasn't altogether ready for it. It raised quite a hullabaloo. But Knox stuck to his ground. He was the eternal optimist. And the university people began to support it."

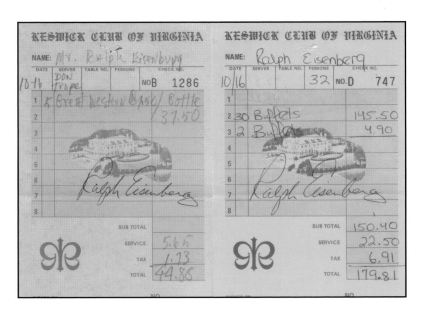

Knox Turnbull had wanted a club that was more open. He didn't care so much about a person's history, but wanted everybody to feel welcome, have fun, and enjoy all kinds of celebrations. Dr. & Mrs Ralph Eisenberg, members at the time, made arrangements for their son Jay's Bar Mitzvah to take place at the club in October of 1971. Their 30 guests enjoyed a buffet supper for which the Eisenbergs paid $4.85 each. The Great Western wine they drank cost $7.50 a bottle. Total gratuity for the event was $28.15. (Receipts courtesy of Jay and Carrie Eisenberg.)

A letter from the club's board of directors, quoted in the *Daily Progress* on June 16, 1972, reminded all members: "Membership in the club is something of value to many of us. It is more than just 18 golf holes, 10 tennis courts, two swimming pools and some dining facilities. It is a social institution with a diversity of membership – economic, political, cultural – that has made it unique certainly in this part of the country." According to that same article, Turnbull's estate "indicated a desire to liquidate the asset and gave the club first refusal of the offer to sell." Ideas for a membership owner plan were discussed with the hope that the club could be kept alive, and a letter to members plainly stated that "either we get 300 [out of then-600 members to agree to the plan] ... or the landlord shuts the club down for the indefinite future." Only 60 members agreed to the original plan, so it went through various revisions, and in a subsequent article dated June 27, 1972, it featured "a significantly reduced investment by members, and a dues structure which differs from previous proposals." But in the end, the money did not come through, the club folded, and no newsletter was printed in August of 1972. Another chapter officially closed.

R.J. Kirchman's rendering of the Villa Crawford was a gift to Chuck Kincannon from his wife Susie. It evokes images of grace and grandeur that are entirely in keeping with the property's original context but for the most part out of sync with the reality of the 1970s and 1980s. (Image courtesy of Chuck & Susie Kincannon.)

76

Chapter 4

Another Go of It, and Another...

After the active, exciting, transformative times of the 1960s and early 1970s, the mansion-turned-clubhouse in Keswick experienced what could be called a has-been period, followed by several enthusiastic attempts to revive operations that did not pan out, leading observers at the time to describe the property as "failed." Mary Ann Elwood, a former club member, noted in an article in the *Charlottesville Daily Progress* on August 7, 1983, "It has a history of doom, a sense of haplessness about it." Dan Genest, who wrote the article, simply stated that the owners "never made the club a lasting venture." Reflective hindsight, however, allows the view that this time period was simply the precursor to the next stage or, to put it another way: Hold on, just hold on through the next number of years – despite various indicators to the contrary, the best is yet to come.

For a few years after the club's doors closed in 1972, there was no single force to drive the business and oversee the extensive property. The original home of Mr. & Mrs. Robert B. Crawford was 60 years old by this time and had served as a clubhouse for 25 years, but during this period, the lower level 19th Hole tavern was the only part of the house officially operating. Stories are told of young people who entered the house of their own accord, made a fire in one of the fireplaces and toasted marshmallows, and in untold ways explored the abandoned spaces of the big old house. Considering that no one was fixing leaks or keeping mice out or in general protecting or maintaining, it is hardly a wonder that the structure and grounds suffered greatly during this time. Locals observed and lamented the empty building, neglected gardens, rusty gates, grassy tennis courts, ragged basketball nets, dilapidating cabanas, as well as the peeling paint, wobbly railings, and fallen plaster in the once grand house. Neighbors tell of riding their horses through tall grass that used to be trimmed lawn.

The golf course also continued to operate during this period. With cart rental, it remained operational as a leased entity during the mid-1970s and was called the Keswick Golf Club. There were still some good times. Don Celec remembers when he and Rod Wilson met there in 1973, and Rod parked his brand new Toyota pickup truck – "a fancy one with big tires," said Celec – by the front portico. They went inside for some drinks, and when they came out, Rod's truck was gone. He was sure someone had stolen it until they saw the tire tracks going down the 10th fairway. The truck had been left in neutral without its emergency brake on and was in the pond at the bottom of the hill.

But even the hold-out golf course suffered a huge blow. In 1977, golf pro Belden MacMillan died a mysterious death in the club's front parking lot. Avery Chenoweth wrote in the *Charlottesville Observer* (May 29-June 3, 1992), "As Stephen King made clear in The Shining, every decent hotel has its share of creepy stories. But while Keswick country club is no Overlook Hotel, it does have one mystery to its morbid credit – an unsolved murder." MacMillan was shot in his truck after letting his wife out so she could get into her own car. "One officer who describes the crime as 'very weird,' says they never established a motive or a suspect." No robbery was involved, no associated vandalism was observed, and to this day the crime remains unsolved.

The Riddervold family moved to Keswick from Norway in 1971. The children, Julius (age 8), Anna Maria (4), and Leif (6), are shown here practicing their putts on the 12th hole in 1973 after the club had closed but the golf course remained operational. (Photo courtesy of Dr. and Mrs. Hans Olav Riddervold.)

"Jefferson and the Virginia Wine Country": A Theme-Resort-Inn (Almost)

1977 was not altogether a tragical year. Northerner (as one from the North was still sometimes called in the South) Bill Lane had his own vision of the property, a vision that involved not only a wonderful place to visit, dine, and play, but also capitalized on an industry just beginning to reemerge in Virginia. The project would also create a connection with Thomas Jefferson, the third President of the United States, whose nearby home, Monticello, had been attracting visitors since it opened as an historic site in 1924.

Lane knew that he and Thomas Jefferson had at least one thing in common: they both

The North American native Norton grape, vitis aestivalis *(above), was well known in the U.S. in the decades before Prohibition, and did in fact produce the "best red wine of all nations" at Vienna World's Fair in 1873. Visionary entrepreneurs a full century later saw once again that Virginia indeed had the potential to produce great wine. Gianni Zonin of Gambellara, Italy, shown here examining a native American grapevine, founded Barboursville Vineyards in 1976, a year before Bill Lane wanted to create a vineyard resort on the Villa Crawford property. (Photo courtesy of Barboursville Vineyards.)*

knew Virginia's potential to be a major player in the wine industry. Jefferson strongly believed that the conditions were right and that the new nation would be wise to limit its dependency on foreign wines. He had boasted in a letter to Monsieur Lasteyrie on July 15, 1808, that "We could, in the United States, make as great a variety of wines as are made in Europe, not exactly of the same kinds, but doubtless as good." Virginia soil, climate, and topography produced excellent wines in the 19th century. In 1873, a Virginia Norton wine was named "best red wine of all nations" at the Vienna World's Fair. Shortly before the Villa Crawford was built, another President – Theodore Roosevelt – gave high praise to a local wine served at a reception at the University of Virginia. Prohibition in the 1920s had dried up the industry, but experimental plantings of vinifera in the 1950s gave rise to renewed interest in local wines.

Six wineries opened in Virginia in the 1970s, including Barboursville Vineyards about 20 miles away. Bill Lane wanted his own lush vineyard to be reminiscent of the French wine regions and he wanted it to be part of a complex where guests could also get every club amenity. His theme, "Jefferson and the Virginia Wine Country," outlined in a report generated by George Davies, vice president of Piedmont Vineyards Company, involved a redesigned Villa Crawford. It was to resemble a Bordeaux estate chateau, and all existing resort facilities – golf course, tennis courts, swimming pools – would be brought "on-stream via formation of semi-private clubs." Additionally, a winery and a "stallion station" would complement the complex.

Lane addressed the existing operations first. He hired 27-year-old Mike Miller, who had been the assistant golf pro at the Fairfax (Virginia) Country Club, to head the golf operation. Miller saw his new position as an opportunity to advance his own career and get in on the ground floor of a promising venture. He considered Bill Lane "a visionary: he imagined this beautiful place, architecturally significant, where wine would be produced and people would come and stay and eat fine food and play golf and play tennis – it would be a destination – ironically, as it is now."

Davies' cash flow analysis noted that "the property continues to maintain a remarkable cash flow given the deplorable condition of the few facilities now in operation," and noted that the fairways had not been fertilized in six years. Nevertheless, during the first six months of 1977, "the Keswick golf operation, related snack bar and cart operation grossed over $116,000." Davies' report noted that "All indications are that the University people would welcome and support a revitalized Keswick operation." The tennis operation would take advantage of the "current tennis boom developed after Keswick lost active management." Pools were operational, but patio areas and locker rooms needed refurbishing. Improved dining facilities in the old Hunt Room would be "the closest major dining facilities to Monticello-Ash Lawn." Mike Miller recalls that Lane hired an eccentric Italian chef named Fausto, whose dynamic personality included singing to the guests.

The old clubhouse was considered "basically sound, but in dire need of decorating, furnishings, and equipment." The 18 guest rooms would be remodeled into 24, with the possibility of an additional 55-room unit. Davies' report stated: "If the existing Keswick facilities can demonstrate sufficient drawing power to the Washington executive market and/or the two-salaried family unit, then additional guest rooms would be added" – another irony, considering Keswick Hall's present drawing power. Lane's goal, according to a *Daily Progress* article on May 11, 1978, was to "bring a more French influence into the architectural feeling" of the house, and remove its central (front) portico, a proposal that met with resistance. Frederick Nichols, a University of Virginia architectural historian, said in the article, "In my view, it is more interesting to keep the character it has, which is more American... after all, the wine they [will] produce is American." This portico remains facing the horizon pool.

Mike Miller was the golf pro in 1978-79 while Bill Lane worked to redesign the club as a vineyard and resort. "When I first came down and looked at the place, I thought 'You've got to be kidding me.' The greens had crabgrass in it – chunks! But he presented this scenario, this grand plan. You look at it, you see his vision, and you take the leap."

Lane's plan included the development of a 100,000-case winery facility with "appropriate attractively styled point-of-sale tasting rooms." This facility would be located near the Keswick exit off Interstate 64 (the Richmond to Charlottesville stretch having been opened just six years earlier in 1971) "for maximum exposure to the 800,000 visitors attracted annually to nearby Monticello." About 35 "showcase" acres of vineyard would be planted at Keswick, with another 500 acres on nearby leased property. The company projected that its "superpremium" wine would generate two million dollars annually, and it expected to become the major producer of grafted vinifers wine stock east of California, with over 5000 root-stock mother plants as foundational material. Also, due to the proximity of the Keswick Hunt Club, as well as the recent move of the Virginia Horse Show Association offices to Charlottesville, Lane's plan included "a 24-box stall stable for the breeding and training of Cleveland Bay crossbred heavy hunters and coach horses."

Bill Lane said in the *Daily Progress* article that his dream was "probably the last chance for Keswick… If this doesn't fly, the property will probably be broken up." But his almost-vineyard was not to be and most of the proposed improvements never materialized. As Mike Miller said, "Bill Lane had the plan. He had the vision. He just didn't have the money." By the end of the summer of 1979, Mike Miller, Fausto, and many others were out of a job. And once again, the Villa Crawford sat empty.

Among many other accomplishments, Thomas Jefferson – third United States President and architect, owner, and resident of nearby Monticello – was a very respectable wine connoisseur. When Monticello itself began to be constructed in 1769, Jefferson was just 26 years old, and he directed that the wine cellar was not only necessary, but also among the first parts of the house to be built. From 1784 to 1789, while he lived in Paris serving as American commissioner, then minister, to France, he learned to appreciate wine even more. In 1787 he took an incognito tour of Burgundy, the Rhône Valley, and Bordeaux – studying, tasting, and learning to discern the subtleties of the finest wines of these areas. His tastes developed, and like any wine enthusiast, he was anxious for others to begin to expand their palates as well.

Owing to the need to preserve wine for long sea voyages, fortified wines from Spain and Portugal such as Madeira and Port had long been staples in the colonies. But changes in bottling techniques allowed Sauternes, Burgundy, and still Champagne to make their way to the newly formed United States, starting with a shipment Jefferson arranged in 1789 for George Washington. Jefferson also served as wine consultant to three subsequent Presidents – Adams, Madison, and Monroe – advising on appropriate table wines for state dinners. For reasons one could enjoy speculating on, Jefferson's congratulatory letter to Monroe included all of three sentences on the election while focusing almost entirely on stocking the White House wine cellar.

Keswick at the Movies

After Bill Lane's operation closed up and throughout the 1979 holiday season, the big old mansion sat alone again. Grand parties, buffet suppers, golf and tennis tournaments, swim meets, wedding receptions, hayrides – all these were images of the past. Chunks of plaster began to fall from the ceilings, and wallpaper hung loosely off the walls. By all accounts, the place was a shambles. Then one evening at the Gaslight Restaurant in downtown Charlottesville, a chance conversation led to a new story. At the bar sat the grown children of the same Donald Stevens who had spearheaded the opening of the Keswick Country Club in 1948. Rosely and Gordon Stevens, whose early childhood was spent largely at the club, were approached that evening by a man who struck up a conversation with them and asked if they might know of a place like an inn that could be used for the filming of a movie.

Did they ever. The building was empty – that was a plus. It was a mess, but that was a detail. Next thing anyone knew, the Villa Crawford had made a place for itself in the archives of Universal Studios.

Since the filming of the motion picture *Giant* in Keswick in 1955, there had not been Hollywood celebrities of this caliber in the neighborhood. Alan Alda, of *M*A*S*H* fame, would be in town in March of 1980 to direct some of the fall scenes of *The Four Seasons*, which starred – besides himself – Carol Burnett, Rita Moreno, Len Cariou, Jack Weston, Bess

In early 1980 Universal Studios filmed fall interior scenes for The Four Seasons *in the Villa Crawford. The movie starred Alan Alda, Carol Burnett, Rita Moreno, Len Cariou, Jack Weston, Bess Armstrong, Sandy Dennis, and the real-life daughters of Alan Alda, Elizabeth and Beatrice. (Image used by permission of Universal Studios.)*

Armstrong, Sandy Dennis, and the real-life daughters of Alan Alda, Elizabeth and Beatrice. The movie portrays three middle aged couples who take a vacation together each season of the year. They drive, eat, and laugh together and weather life's storms along the way. One of the men makes a decision that introduces a new character and dramatically changes the whole dynamic. The decision forces the other characters to examine their viewpoints and their relationships, and the process which leads everyone to new discoveries about life and each other.

The fall scene finds them at a country inn in what looks like New England. Alda agreed that the old Keswick clubhouse would work well for the interior shots (a completely different building was used for the exterior shots). The large spaces and tall ceilings of main floor served perfectly as a movie set. During the film, while guests check in at the registration desk, the present day Villa library can be seen in the background while numerous extras are milling around. The "inn's" busy dining room was set in the present day snooker room, and the couples have a lively dinner at a round table there with the Villa staircase balusters plainly visible through the doorway. The staircase itself and the hallway on the second floor gave Alan Alda and Jack Weston a place to walk while in somewhat heated discussion. Room 12, in the northwest corner of the second floor, was used as a guest room for the scene of the mother-daughter talk between Carol Burnett and Elizabeth Alda. And the Villa Crawford's main hall and grand staircase served as the scene of one of the movie's most awkward moments.

The film crew utterly transformed the four rooms and the second floor hallway to meet their needs. It was a temporary and most definitely partial face lift for the clubhouse. As with any movie set, all that mattered was what the camera would capture. Whatever angle it would face, these surfaces – and these surfaces only – were plastered, painted or papered. Room 12 was a great example of this. Every bit of wall, ceiling and floor within the scope of the camera's lens was remodeled to beautifully reflect the style of the inn, and every bit that was out of its scope, i.e., behind and next to the camera, was left in shabby condition.

Within a few weeks, the film crew and actors came and went. The voices, movement, and purpose they had brought with them gave way to a different kind of silence when they left. It was a silence more solid, more weighted with experience. The Villa Crawford itself, so clearly the set of the fall interior scenes in *The Four Seasons* to anyone who has walked through it – seemed touched with the kind of immortality that comes by mere association with a Hollywood movie. Or so it seems in retrospect.

Reynolds Roost

Dottie Reynolds wanted to spruce up every room in the clubhouse-turned-movie-set, including the laughable ones she found with half of the walls newly papered. She wanted guests to enjoy nice dinners, golfers to enjoy the course, and swimmers to enjoy the pool. She and her husband Glenn, who had been the club's PGA golf professional during the active and thriving years of Turnbull's ownership, wanted their own dream to take wing. Just a few weeks after the Universal Studios crew packed up and departed, Glenn and Dottie Reynolds, next in line, took their turn at running a country club here again.

Since the would-be winery venture of Bill Lane, the property had been in the hands of the Drum Financial Corporation of Omaha, Nebraska, which controlled any contracts relating to the use of the property until an actual sale would occur. According to a *Charlottesville Daily Progress* article on April 30, 1980, William H. Burress, president of Burress Land and Lumber Company of Lynchburg, Virginia, had his eye on the entire Keswick property, but the Reynolds wanted the golf course. A loose understanding existed that once Burress bought the old country club, he would sell the golf course to the Reynolds.

The Reynolds family proceeded undaunted. Regarding the new venture and despite the challenges they would face, Glenn admitted to Kip Coons in that *Daily Progress* article, "I'm excited." Dottie Reynolds, noting that his remark was "the understatement of the year," added that "It's been a dream of ours for a long time." They knew all about good times at the Keswick Club of Virginia, and wanted, this go-round, to make it "Reynolds Roost" – a family

Glenn and Dottie Reynolds with their granddaughter Mindy, as shown in a promotional pamphlet for the newly opened Keswick Country Club. (Photo courtesy of Glenn and Dottie Reynolds.)

affair that would include their two sons, Tim and Dave, in the daily operations. Glenn, who had become club pro in Pen Park in Charlottesville after the Keswick Club folded in 1972, would be the director of golf; Dottie would coordinate all of the administrative as well as the catering and banquet aspects of the business; Tim, who was at that time an assistant pro at the Roanoke

Glenn and Dottie Reynolds knew what they were getting into, and the aerial photographs their sons took of every square acre in the spring of 1980 proved it. This photograph shows the back six tennis courts grown over and unusable, and the swimming pools obviously empty and dirty. The Reynolds spruced up the building and grounds, and ran the operation as a family for two and a half years. (Photo courtesy of Tim and Dave Reynolds.)

(Virginia) Country Club, would become head golf pro; and Dave would be the course superintendent.

The 18-hole par 73 course opened to the public on Wednesday, May 7, 1980, and included "a full instructional program, practice tees, putting greens and carts in top condition." Glenn Reynolds had always had great respect for the course. "It's a beautiful golf course and beautiful country," he said. "It's a great layout. The small greens and length make it really tough, and the front side is pretty tight. No one has set it on fire. I think the course record is still 67." Other facilities available to the public were the driving range, the pools, the tennis courts ("three clay courts and one all-weather court... set amidst towering trees"), and of course the "19th Hole" snack bar, "offering patrons a choice of indoor or outdoor dining in a relaxed informal atmosphere" from noon till early evening. The Reynolds also continued the tradition of the Jefferson Country Golf Tournament, and the *Daily Progress* covered this event as they had covered numerous others. On Saturday, August 14, 1982, Chuck Baker remembers he trailed Duane Bickers for the lead in this tournament, and "was six shots behind with nine holes to play on Sunday, but rallied to win."

In the fall of 1982, despite the many improvements they had made to the house and property, the bubble burst for the Reynolds family when they received official word that the future of the club would not include them. They were given two weeks to abandon the operation.

Lynchburg businessman William Burress, the new owner, planned to sell house lots around the golf course and possibly develop the clubhouse into a small corporate conference center, according to Chuck Kincannon, the real estate agent who handled the transaction, in a *Daily Progress* article of April 3, 1981. But plans stalled and time went by. Burress leased the Keswick Golf Club to Eric V. Bartoli in January of 1983. Bartoli advertised for memberships for $250.00, but by July of that year, according to an August 7, 1983, article in the *Daily Progress*, Bartoli's firm, with lawsuits pending, "voluntarily" closed the doors, and a green "Closed" sign was taped to the clubhouse door – found by a golfer who said he came early to beat the crowds. The club in Keswick had closed its doors again. What else was new?

Five Years Trying

Within a very short time, the neglected Keswick course was in dismal condition. Danny Finnegan reported in the *Charlottesville Daily Progress* on August 5, 1984, that "Walking along what used to be fairways you feel more like you are walking on a battlefield than a championship golf course with old sand traps looking more like bomb craters." Bunkers were ant-infested, sand traps were overrun with vegetation, and it looked to Finnegan like someone had seriously over-fertilized the greens to the point of absolute ruin. George O'Brien, a golf pro who owned two courses in New Jersey, saw its potential and wanted in. "The golf course has integrity. It's a damn shame they let it go," he said in the article. William Burress sold the property for $1.5 million in July of 1984 to O'Brien, who set up a partnership with Thomas Curtis, a Houston developer.

O'Brien immediately began revitalizing the course, a plan that involved resurfacing the greens, reseeding with Pencross (a type of bent grass), and installing seven miles of piping for a new watering system. Curtis focused on the rest of the property, and alarmed the county supervisors, planning commission, and area residents by proposing hundreds of homes and some commercial development – locals all feared a negative impact on the area's character, to say nothing of groundwater supplies. The developers reduced the plan's scope and promised that the necessary infrastructure would accompany any development, but intense opposition remained.

By December, 1985, O'Brien was out of the picture despite his $1 million investment, and one of the biggest names in golf – Arnold Palmer – was in, along with plans for an elaborate resort with a $25 million price tag and fewer residences. On Friday, December 13, 1985, "Arnie's Army" gathered at the Omni Hotel in downtown Charlottesville to hear about the "Curtis-Palmer Venture." Palmer told the crowd of 600 well-wishers, "It's going to be a very sophisticated

In July of 1984, Thomas Curtis, shown opposite, partnered with George O'Brien in an attempt to revive the club. By the time this photo was taken for an article in the Daily Progress *on February 27, 1986, O'Brien was out of the picture and Arnold Palmer was in. Curtis said in the article, "I don't see my idea as being any different. I'm just doing it the right way." By early 1990, however, he owed $18 million to 30 creditors and the case was in bankruptcy court. (Charlottesville Daily Progress *photo by Jim Carpenter.)*

development," and described an extensive project that he expected would someday bring a PGA sanctioned tournament to the course.

Several roadblocks again kept the project from moving forward. Curtis had personal legal issues, for one thing, though in a *Daily Progress* article on February 27, 1986, he stated that he was trying to resolve these "as quickly as possible." He diverted attention by focusing on the latest site plan until water – or lack thereof – stood in the way. Project manager Timothy Riggle said the water issue would delay the opening of the new exclusive golf resort until spring of 1988. But then money became the issue – various lawsuits against Curtis in 1987 as well as the 1988 bankruptcy of the savings and loan that financed his project. The property had become an eyesore, and the considerable lack

of community optimism didn't help either. Blame and circumstance aside, Curtis continued to push plans forward. In a *Daily Progress* article on May 29, 1989, he said, "We're doing what is necessary to complete the project... The completion of the project is the only thing that will convince the public."

Completion seemed less and less likely with every passing month, evidenced by piles of dirt all over the course, wild grass growing in the oval pool, boarded up windows, and cracked retaining walls. By early 1990, Thomas Curtis owed $18 million to 30 creditors, and the case was in bankruptcy court. On April 9, 1990, an offer to buy the property for $5.5 million came through from an interested but initially unnamed buyer, followed naturally by strong discussion about how to divide the money among the creditors. The accounting firm representing the buyer, based in London, did not at that time stir up excitement about the future of the club. Even after the purchase took place five months later on September 17, 1990, not much came forth except a somewhat mild statement that the old clubhouse could open as a luxury country inn within two years along with, finally, the name of the buyer.

A *Daily Progress* article on December 8, 1990, entitled "Keswick Country Club is on the mend," noted that the architectural firm Browne, Eichman, Dalgliesh, Gilpin & Paxton had been hired by the Keswick Acquisition Corporation, and thus the tide came in. The Keswick Acquisition Corporation represented Ashley Inns, which happened to be owned

These two photos, the first from 1986 and the second from 1988, show one aspect of Curtis' plan: he did not intend to remove the oval pool, but rather to fill it and make an earth mound over top. No wonder wild grass was growing in it. (Charlottesville Daily Progress photos by John Strader, above, and Starke Jett, below.)

by Sir Bernard Ashley, widower of Laura Ashley and head of the immense firm that they had built together. Winston Churchill did say: "Success is the ability to go from failure to failure without losing your enthusiasm." The property's 'Life Full of Failures,' as recounted in the *Daily Progress* in August of 1983, was about to see success. Its potential could not, would not, be denied. History had shown that at any given time, someone was envisioning its long-term viability, someone was not giving up. This time, the someone had a personal fortune and an undeniable knack for getting things done.

The site plan Curtis put forth in 1986 included a total of 48 guest rooms (ironically, the current number): a conference center with 22 guest rooms constructed to match the Villa Crawford; a lodge/fitness center with 20 guest rooms to be located at the site of the deteriorating oval, steel pool; and six guest suites within the original clubhouse. The two new buildings would be connected to the old Villa Crawford – the main clubhouse – by covered walkways. A posh restaurant, 70 home sites, and the renovated golf course, seven outdoor tennis courts, one platform tennis court, jogging and riding trails, a croquet lawn, and both an indoor and an outdoor pool were also part of the plan, which was scheduled to be ready for guests by spring or summer of 1987. (Image courtesy of Winkie Motley, Keswick Life.*)*

The Villa Crawford looked like this in 1990 when Sir Bernard Ashley flew over the Virginia countryside to consider its possibilities. He looked beyond the obvious – an old mansion in a sad state of disrepair. Instead, he envisioned a magnificent "country house" hotel integrating the Villa Crawford into a grand design of perfect elegance and comfort. Over the next few years he led a dedicated team that transformed it into a world-class destination. Keswick Hall opened in August of 1993. (Photo by J.T. Anesi; courtesy of Charlottesville Daily Progress.*)*

Chapter 5

A Country House Hotel

The property in Keswick that Sir Bernard Ashley purchased in September of 1990 was both a challenge and a treasure. Local author Avery Chenoweth described it well: "For years now the old Keswick clubhouse has sat back among the huge old trees of its property like some relic from *Tender is the Night* lost in the landscape of William Faulkner. It's a big pale yellow palace, rather grandiose in its dereliction. Its broken-windowed silence used to evoke the lost atmosphere of all the big parties and golf tournaments that once filled its windows with lights and the driveway with cars and people.... Indeed, for anyone who relishes a mansion of senile ruin, the old club was a wonderful place to visit – a sort of local Manderlay. The swimming pool was crumbling, with trees growing up from its cracked floor, windows punched out, gaping doors. And yet the touches of elegance remained. Local architect Henry Browne, whose firm designed the renovations, says that until recently, even in its disuse, the place still had silver light switches and silver switch plates – which sadly vanished, he says."

Manderlay, the grand English country house in Daphne du Maurier's *Rebecca*, mirrored the Villa Crawford not only in having been at one time lovely and later left in ruin. Both mansions, in their prime, boasted extensive grounds and gardens, exquisite furnishings, impeccable attention to service, and a rich history. Both, after their own various tragedies, were the subject of much reminiscing and lamentation. Neither, by any stretch of imagination, was ordinary. When the Villa Crawford came back to life as part of a "country house hotel," it came back on a much greater scale to its original life as a country house and was once again decidedly extraordinary. It came back in good part because a young architect was paying attention.

A Country House Hotel

Robert L. Paxton, an architect with Browne, Eichman, Dalgliesh & Gilpin, the same Charlottesville firm that had done design work for Thomas Curtis in the 1980s, simply followed up with an idea he had. In the *Charlottesville/Albemarle Business Observer Magazine* of July 16-22, 1992, Paxton said, "I read the article which mentioned Sir Bernard's project in Wales, Llangoed Hall, where he renovated a historic country estate as an inn.... We knew the strengths of Keswick, and we knew how any problems could be overcome. The Keswick property with its Italianate villa dating from the early 20th century was perfect for Sir Bernard's concept of bringing the English Country House to the United States." Paxton then kept going where most people might have stopped – he wrote a proposal and sent it off.

Steve Mitchell, vice president for development of Ashley House, who later had responsibility of overseeing construction on the Keswick property, said in the same article, "I don't know how Bob's letter and proposal reached the top of a huge pile of correspondence. Perhaps his perseverance, but somehow we came here to look at Keswick."

Sir Bernard Ashley was no stranger to grand homes and beautiful designs. Beginning at their kitchen table in the early 1950s with a foray into block-printing fabrics, Laura and Bernard Ashley subsequently hit upon a style that developed throughout the next several decades into a fashion and home furnishings empire – and a fortune. In the 1980s they had had the idea to open "country house hotels," which would give them another avenue for their interior design

Sir Bernard Ashley purchased Llangoed Hall in Wales (above) in 1987, The Inn at Perry Cabin on the Chesapeake Bay (below) in 1989, and the Keswick property in 1990, and converted all of them to country house hotels. In 1999, the Inn at Perry Cabin and Keswick Hall were both sold to Orient-Express.

expertise, showcase their products, and increase their profile. However, Laura Ashley died in 1985 after falling down a flight of stairs on her 60th birthday, a very tragic and shocking event. A couple of years later, Bernard Ashley carried on with the idea himself, and as with everything, did it in his inimitable fashion.

In 1987 Ashley was awarded the title of Knight Bachelor by the Queen, and began focusing his efforts on the hotel business, first with Llangoed Hall in Wales, and followed by the Inn at Perry Cabin on the Chesapeake Bay in Maryland. When the Keswick property was being considered, B.A., as Sir Bernard was called, flew with his team to survey the house and land. "We came by helicopter the first time," recalled Phyllis Koch, design director. "I freaked out – I thought it had to be haunted." Walls were indeed crumbling, windows were broken and boarded, and plaster was falling from the ceiling when they got inside. Every bit of the plaster moldings would have to be recreated.

But B.A.'s impression was different, and his vision was impressive. "When I first saw Virginia," he said in the *Albemarle* magazine of February/March 1993, "I was amazed – flying over this country was just incredible, it was so beautiful. I just fell in love with it. And what I wanted to create here was more of a home, more of a club than a commercial enterprise. I wanted to combine all the best elements of the American way of life. I like the country, I'm not a town person, and I'm not interested in six-lane highways. We're targeting people who like the same way of life that I like: Settled out in the country, a comfortable club...like the furniture – we don't use incredibly rare antiques, but it's furniture you can be comfortable in."

This image of Sir Bernard during the construction phase of Keswick Hall portrays him as many remember him – a regular guy, relaxed, enjoying himself. Those who worked with him invariably spoke very highly of him. (Photo courtesy of Phyllis Koch.)

Before the project got started, steps were taken to confirm the possibility of success, including an assessment of what the neighbors would think. Libby Wilson recalled that on a visit to the Inn at Perry Cabin, she and her husband Bob were called into the office and asked what they thought about the project. "Donald Stevens had been a real entrepreneur," she said she told them, "but in general this neighborhood was pretty anti-development. However, these are gracious people, very well endowed for the most part, and will support you."

The Charlottesville Daily Progress on December 8, 1990, described the venture simply and cautiously as "the latest attempt to revive the troubled Keswick Club." B. A. accepted that the country club operation and the surrounding real estate came with the package. In the early 1990s, moreover, despite his notoriety, which gave him great advantage over the string of unsuccessful predecessors, and despite his substantial resources, meaning no loan, no debt, and no bank pressuring for profits, this business plan seemed to need more than the country house hotel itself. All three, it was determined – hotel, club and estate – would contribute proportionally for long term profitability.

The golf course was addressed first. Arnold Palmer was brought back into the picture, and work began in early December of 1990. Peter McDonough, Keswick Hall's golf course superintendent and longest-standing employee, came to the property about six months later to interview for a job. "I used to work for Mr. Palmer. He said, 'You're going here.' Yes, sir. 'You'll like it, trust me.' Yes, sir." McDonough found the oval pool and dilapidated cabanas still in place in May, 1991, though the Olympic length pool was already gone. "Those cabanas weren't in great shape in the 60s, and by the 90s they were thoroughly rotted. Decrepit is a good word," he said. He came back a month later, in June, to start work; by then, the oval pool and cabanas had also been removed. "My first week at Keswick was extremely challenging. They had the golf course 80% completed without having Army Corps of Engineer permits, no ponds, water wasn't installed, no electricity, no pumps, no grass, no anything, just dirt and awful erosion." These details had evidently not bothered B.A., nor was he daunted by the failures of previous owners. In a *Daily Progress* article on June 24, 1992, he said, "The golf course was

One of the first agenda items was to remove the oval pool. Above, in the spring of 1991, Jake Eubanks of Coiners Scrap Iron begins the laborious process of cutting through the quarter-inch thick steel to remove the old oval pool in sections. To the right, spreading sand not for a bunker, but to prepare the base for one of the greens, Doug Moore contributed to the Arnold Palmer's redesign of the Keswick golf course. (Charlottesville Daily Progress *photos by Jim Carpenter.)*

The golf course was redesigned to be a par 71 of just over 6000 yards. The main change compared to the original Fred Findlay course first opened in 1949 was that the nines were flip-flopped. In this long view (above) showing the partially finished clubhouse and hotel, Peter McDonough confers with Arnold Palmer on the nearly finished 11th fairway; grassing work was done, but trees still needed to be planted. (Photo courtesy of Peter McDonough.)

On September 23, 1992, Sir Bernard Ashley and Arnold Palmer observe and celebrate the newly opened golf course. Lady Regine Ashley, second wife of Sir Bernard, stands next to her husband. Laura Ashley passed away in 1985, well before the purchase of the property. (Charlottesville Daily Progress photo by M. Gentry.)

nearly finished....We could see that with a little bit of effort we could get a project going."

About a year after McDonough's arrival, on May 19, 1992, welcome news came for those who had long lamented the lack of a decent Keswick course. The *Daily Progress* reported that the Ashley group had just made Arnold Palmer the first Honorary Founding Member. News of an actual, playable course couldn't be far behind. "We've tried to combine a little of the links atmosphere with the country club golf," Palmer said in the article. "I think we've been successful in doing that. It won't be an overly long course, but it's longer than people think. We have holes that maybe you can't hit with a driver. So I think the distance is going to be academic. It will be a test for the better player." On September 23, 1992, the official opening of the new Arnold Palmer signature golf course was celebrated, with Palmer, B.A., and Lady Regine Ashley, B.A.'s second wife, in attendance. The "good bones" of the Fred Findlay course that had first opened in 1949, its established layout and old growth trees, meant that Palmer's focus had been on changing details such as tee box locations, bunkering, shaping of greens, contouring of fairways, and selecting turfgrass varieties for playability and climate conditions. Three elements differed fundamentally from the old course: The nines were flip-flopped, the almost-always dry course now had a water supply – an 18-million gallon lake – that would keep it beautifully green, and golf memberships were rather more expensive – now $25,000 per individual by invitation only plus an annual $1,200 fee.

"Saving" the Villa Crawford

Sir Bernard felt strongly that the Villa Crawford itself held an important place in the overall scheme. "It all flowed," McDonough said. "B.A.'s point was that everything was going to flow through the Villa Crawford. It was important to him. That's why they seamed it instead of bulldozing it, and spent probably ten times the amount of money to save it." With the topiary garden and gazebo – a prime location for weddings – flowing out the portico to the north (where the horizon pool is now located), as well as the clubhouse in that direction, and the new section of the hotel continuing as it does toward the south, the Villa Crawford's prominent position can be understood. The old extension to the south, with its porch, administrative offices, kitchen, and Hunt Room, was too dilapidated and therefore torn down, but the rest of the mansion was covered in plastic for four and a half months – six weeks to remove the asbestos that wrapped every pipe within the walls as a protection against freezing, and three more months to make sure there was no contamination. All that time, only authorized workers

Sir Bernard Ashley determined that the integrity of the original mansion should be preserved and that the Villa Crawford would become the heart of the hotel; therefore only its back extension was razed during construction in 1991. The remainder was wrapped in plastic for four and a half months during the asbestos removal process, after which the renovation and expansion work proceeded. The second story right hand corner windows belong to Room 9, the original master bedroom of the house; the room beneath it is now the hotel's bar. (Photo courtesy of Peter McDonough.)

Integrating the old Villa Crawford into the overall structure allowed for a true 100-year anniversary celebration to occur in 2012. Above, construction of the hotel during the winter of 1991-92 continued despite the weather. (Photo courtesy of Phyllis Koch.)

in hazmat suits were allowed in. But as with the golf course, much of the original integrity was maintained. Without a doubt, B.A.'s directive ultimately allowed for a true 100-year anniversary and historic designation in 2012.

Sir Bernard confirmed his vision in a *Daily Progress* article on June 24, 1992. The hotel, he said, would address the "distressingly impersonal" aspects of most other hotels he had visited, which were "about as comfortable as an airline terminal." Ashley House marketing materials declared that the pleasures and comforts of such a property were meant to create "the best of two worlds: a British Edwardian household with European service and Virginia hospitality," and the accommodations in the new 48-room inn were meant to make guests feel "as though they were visiting a fine home, where service would be unobtrusive." An early hotel fact sheet described "an abundance of public rooms, galleries, salons and ante rooms for the relaxation and social enjoyment of guests, the total absence of anything commercial either by design or nature (thus no traditional bar or restaurant), overall ambiance of warmth and intimacy with a lived-in quality that is totally reminiscent of a private residence or house, highly personalized service with anticipation of guest needs being of paramount importance, attention to detail and commitment to excellence in every aspect of the household, and outstanding cuisine and a well stocked wine cellar."

An Inventory-Driven Design Process

During the three-year project that culminated with the opening of the hotel in August of 1993, Phyllis Koch had her work cut out for her. She had 48 guest rooms and all of the public rooms to decorate, every one with its own individual decorating scheme – no fabric, wall covering, or theme was repeated – to say nothing of the show home built as a model for the hotel to come *and* the clubhouse. To accomplish this, a massive inventory was done of two huge warehouses of Laura Ashley fabrics and wall coverings, many of which were offered only in Europe and only in the designer line. The overall decorating plan was based on how much of this or that was available –

Interior designer Phyllis Koch designed 48 guest rooms and all the public spaces in Keswick Hall. One of the most popular for coffee was the morning room (left), so named because of its eastern exposure. It became the hotel's bar about 10 years later. In the main "Crawford Lounge" (above), painted bright yellow, afternoon tea was served buffet style every day along with a bottle of sherry. Since there was no bar per se, a member of the wait staff would promptly oblige if a guest wanted any other drink. (Photos by Philip Beaurline.)

John Bartell, shown here in the show home walking underneath one of the murals he painted, was a street artist from London brought in to paint murals in the hotel, including those on the room-dividing panels between the dining rooms on the lower level. The show home was later sold as a private home. (Photo courtesy of Phyllis Koch.)

definitely an "inventory-driven" process, according to Koch. Despite the challenge, "I had the best time working on this project," she said. "B.A. and his family were so much fun to work with."

Nick Ashley, creative director of both the hall and the show home, and put in charge by his father, echoed her sentiments. "I worked with a fantastic team who were totally professional and wonderful," he said. "I have fond memories of my many trips across the Atlantic to check on progress." The million-dollar showcase home constructed on the estate, also called the "spec house," had several ties to the past. "The Villa Crawford was our cue," said Paxton in the *Observer* magazine of July 16-22, 1992. "It was built in the Italianate manner of the early 1900s." Both the show home and the Villa Crawford were stuccoed, tile-roofed, 8000-square-foot houses built in the favored style of Thomas Jefferson.

In the hotel itself, guest room themes ranged from lawn sports to Italian Renaissance to 1930s Art Deco, and decorations included anything that enhanced and supported the room's particular theme: family photographs, trophies, tackle, watering cans, antique books, globes, baskets, pots, walking sticks, framed sheet music, lace work, shells, birdcages, crystal, etc. Some of these items were bought locally, and some, especially items such as armoires, were purchased abroad – a complicated process, but one which took advantage of the favorable exchange rate at the time and added tremendously to the uniqueness of the hotel's collection. Koch had two buyers in London to whom she sent photographs of the room layouts along with specifications about size, style, and budget for the needed items. In pre-email days, information was mailed back and forth across the Atlantic using the postal service; the buyers scouted around until they found something suitable, exchanged details, and waited for the go-ahead to purchase. Some elements were created especially for the hotel. John Bartell, a street artist from London, was brought in to paint the murals on the room-dividing panels downstairs.

Brief Descriptions of Original Keswick Hall Guest Rooms

Room 1: Italian Renaissance (green, white, blue; ceramics and pots)

Room 2: French Country (blue, tan, orange; pine and fruitwood; walking sticks)

Room 3: Hunt & Dog (hunt green, crimson; cherry woods; trophies, ribbons)

Room 4: Lawn Sport (green and white stripe; red cherry; team photos)

Room 5: Butterfly (white, blue; painted pine; jars and nets)

Room 6: Alba Rose (yellow, white; dark walnut, cherry woods)

Room 7: Wellington (Classic Laura Ashley pineapple motif bed)

Room 8: Swedish (yellow; pickled pine, clocks, wood carvings)

Room 9: Louis XV (painted antique furniture, mirrors)

Room 10: White & Rose (Classic Laura Ashley, bird's eye maple, urns)

Room 11: Bird (lavender, white; birdcages, bird watching pictures)

Room 12: Aviation (queen sleigh bed; planes, caps, trophies, badges)

Room 13: Fishing (green, beige; bleached pine, tackle collection)

Room 14: Italian Country (dark green, beige; ceramic ware and jugs)

Room 15: Jane Austin (pink & white plaid; white painted antiques; books)

Room 16: Blue Toile (blue, gold; watering cans, pitchers)

Room 17: 1930s Art Deco (peach, beige; French doors, iron rail)

Room 18: Fruit (purple, green, white with grape clusters; French, formal)

Room 19: Antique Fan & China (cowslip yellow, green, white; dark wood)

Room 20: Tennis (rose, green, white; white wicker; tennis collections)

Room 21: Maps (brown, rust, green, tan; maps, globes, books)

Room 22: Vegetable (white, brown, beige; baskets, gardening tools, wicker)

Room 23: Nautical (black & white stripe; water skis and oars)

Room 24: Print Room (black, white, beige; black & white prints)

Room 1

Room 25: French Provencal - (rose, white; clocks, crystal)

Room 26: French Provencal - (blue, gold; caning, bells, tassels)

Room 27: Adamesque (teal, white, orange; dark cherry and mahogany)

Room 28: French Topiary (cowslip yellow, periwinkle; cactus, terra cotta)

Room 29: Regency Toy (crimson, green, white; dark cherry and mahogany)

Room 30: Herbs (green, white, tan; dried flowers, herbs, wicker)

Room 31: Swedish/Angel (white, gray, pink; antique radios)

Room 32: Washington Architectural (black & white; black dark wood, columns)

Room 33: Swedish (yellow & white plaid; pots, bowls, bicycles)

Room 34: Cozy Cottage (blue & white plaid; lightwood antiques; teapots)

Room 35: Music (yellow, white, green; musical instruments, framed sheet music)

Room 36: Rowing (brown, rust, navy, burgundy; rattan, b&w crew team photos, oars)

Room 37: Traditional English (red/white cherry blossom; English landscapes)

Room 38: Petit Point (white painted wood, lacework, perfumes)

Room 39: Little French Girls (white and pink; lanterns)

Room 40: French Formal (pink, green, ivory; dark cherry wood; china collection)

Room 41: Shell (blue, white; white furniture, dark mahogany wood, shells)

Room 42: Country House (pink, green; birdcages, china, baskets)

Room 43: Classic Laura Ashley (lavender, white; twin sleigh beds)

Room 44: Miss Dora's House (white, green, mauve; dark walnut, Victorian)

Room 45: Sports (brown, rust, gold, navy; golf and lawn sports)

Room 46: Floral (greens, yellow, pink; dark wood antiques)

Room 47: Antique Glass (pink and white; light woods)

Room 48: Regency (gray and white; black wood antiques)

Room 19 (Photos by Philip Beaurline.)

Liz Ratcliffe, who was chief financial officer for Ashley House Hotels, was part of the project management team, as was Grant Howlett, Keswick Hall's first general manager. They were sent by B.A. to an 'attic auction' at Castle Howard in Sheffield, England, managed by Sothebys, to assist in the acquisition of items for the hotel, clubhouse, and show home. They successfully bid on numerous items, including a pair of garden statues recognizable to *Brideshead Revisited* aficionados who fondly recall the BBC series that had been filmed at Castle Howard; these statues add both weight and whimsy to the lower terrace to this day. Additionally, the contents of the Ashley's town house in Brussels was destined for Keswick, including its sizable antiques collection. Martin Wood's lovely 2009 book, *Laura Ashley*, shows images of that property's salon and library, and nearly every element of those rooms has been enjoyed by Keswick Hall guests ever since, including draperies, furniture, paintings, busts, and mirrors. All of these items and materials were shipped to Keswick in forty 40-foot containers and found new locations, mostly in public areas of the hotel, to grace with their presence.

Undoubtedly, B.A.'s extraordinary and eclectic collection was one important element that invited peaceful meanderings and relaxing teatimes throughout the hotel. Early Ashley House literature stated: "The Ashley genius of interpreting the past to bring beauty and comfort to the present is lavished on the furnishings and decorations of the rooms." To this day, guests take time to stare at the 19th century *Lady with Feathered Hat*, for example, with her gloved hand holding a monocle, and the 19th century white marble bust of a woman in neoclassical attire. They ask about the two portraits framing the entrance to the library, one of a Spanish noblewoman (possibly the Queen of Spain) and one of a Spanish nobleman (possibly the King of Spain). A framed engraving of Napoleon looks over the shoulder of a bust of the Duke of Wellington; for amusement, B.A. left a characteristic bicorne hat on the Duke's head. Many works of art, including an early 19th century portrait of a family with six children, the marble-topped Louis XV style console, the mahogany sideboard with its arched, beaded apron, and the bucolic landscape paintings have always added immensely, if subtly, to the overall pleasure of visiting.

This statue and its counterpart on the lower terrace have been part of the Keswick landscape since they arrived in one of the forty 40-foot containers that brought antiques and other furnishings from Great Britain to Keswick Hall in the early 1990s. These statues came from Castle Howard, where they were, now and then, a part of the background in the BBC Brideshead Revisited *series. (Photo courtesy of Jen Fariello.)*

Soft Opening

In August of 1993 Keswick Hall had its "soft opening," as described by Howlett in the October 1993 edition of *Keswick Life*. Despite the $195 to $645 per night cost, word of mouth was relied upon to fill the rooms -- everything having been set up so that guests would feel like they were visiting a grand country estate for the weekend. Anne Hooff, marketing manager for the three Ashley House properties, explained in a *Richmond-Times Dispatch* article of February 26, 1995, "That's his philosophy, that you've come to his home. He just doesn't happen to be here." Lois Perschetz, who visited early in 1995 and wrote about it in the *Baltimore* magazine in April of 1995, put it a way that has been echoed many times over: "Sir Bernard's vision (we are already on a first-name basis), we are told, was to create a country house in the landed-gentry tradition: Our host is away, but he has graciously loaned us his home and his staff. Thank you, Sir Bernard!"

When guests arrived at either the east gate of the property or the west gate (shown here), they were greeted by the gatekeeper, who ascertained their name and subsequently informed hotel personnel of the arrival. Guests were then warmly greeted by name at the door. The entire arrival process was designed to create a gracious, inviting welcome. (Photo by Philip Beaurline.)

The gatekeeper at the entrance to the property greeted guests first, then alerted hotel personnel of their arrival. An attendant who looked like a butler met the guests as they drove around the circle, greeted them by name, helped them out of their car, and graciously escorted them through the great hall, with its thick, terra cotta floor tiles looking as authentically antique and European as they are. The absence of a registration desk affirmed the grand country estate feeling. "We find ourselves in a gracious public space, full of overstuffed furniture and wonderful antiques," said Perschetz. "The fire is blazing, the table is stacked with books. No desk, no official check-in." Once the guests felt settled, they could mosey on down to one of the common areas, like various living rooms each with its own theme, design, and color scheme. All meals were served in the lower level dining rooms – the dividable space now used for special groups and functions.

A new caliber of cuisine came to Keswick. The fondue nights of the late 1960s became "Sizzling Hot Jazz Barbeques" in the summer of 1994 – Thursday nights meant lavish spreads of barbequed meats, poultry and seafood with sumptuous accompaniments, all set to a different jazz quartet or quintet every week. A traditional brunch was served every Sunday, and the chef hosted special "cookery demonstration luncheons." One advertisement in *Keswick Life* stated that the luncheon "commences at 10:30 AM and includes a tour of Keswick Hall, an hour long demonstration by Chef [Richard] Smith and his team, a three course luncheon with accompanying wine, coffee and petits fours, a comprehensive demonstration, and a recipe pack" for $45.

As might be expected in a lovely

Phyllis Richman, a food critic writing for The Washington Post Magazine *on July 26, 1994, said, "The dining room is a glory of chalk-white walls with a dozen immense arched French doors. Venetian glass chandeliers seems to float over the tables, which are set with white tapers in tall silver candlesticks. Muted pastel undercloths and upholstery offer the only color. Except for the flowers, of course." Candlelight flickered in the series of small mirrors that ran horizontally around the walls about mid height. Dinner at that time cost $55 regardless, plus wine. About afternoon tea, she wrote, "As I ate the scones with the thick, tart lemon jam, I thought to myself, this is worth a two-hour drive." (Photo by Philip Beaurline.)*

Lawrence and Jack Boocock grew up on a prominent farm in Keswick called Castalia. Their portrait, painted in 1909, hangs prominently in the Villa Crawford and strongly reflects the Keswick community's longstanding equestrian tradition. Their father, Murray Boocock, had been one of the founding members of the Keswick Hunt Club in 1896.

country estate, house tours complemented the experience for many visitors, and at least once, revealed the true source of a piece of artwork. During one early tour of the lovely new hotel, as the guide was pointing out the enormous 1909 portrait of two boys in riding habit that currently hangs in the Villa Crawford, club member Norma Flanders listened with interest. Scott Goss, grandson of the younger of the two boys in the painting, related the story as follows: "The guide was saying that this interesting painting had come from France and started to suggest who the boys were. Norma said, 'I beg to differ. I've seen that picture thousands of times.' The tour guide looked incredulously at her and said, 'That can't possibly be so,' and Norma said, 'But it is, it is, it is!'"

The oil on canvas portrait features the Boocock brothers at ages 12 and 9. Lawrence and John Carrol (Jack) grew up and lived for many years at Castalia, a prominent Keswick farm that included a 42-room, 3-story mansion with 14' ceilings. Colonel Lewellyn Flanders and his wife Norma had been frequent visitors at Castalia, and knew the story of their family. Murray and Miriam Boocock, parents of Lawrence and Jack, bought the 670-acre estate in 1895 as a summer home from the Meriwether Lewis family (of Lewis & Clark fame). Murray Boocock was a founding member of the Keswick Hunt Club, begun in 1896, which explains the boys' attire in the portrait. Lawrence and Jack were required by H. Stanley Todd, the artist, to pose two to three times a week for about a month, after which they apparently begged their mother not to make them do that again. The portrait hung in Castalia's main dining room for more than 70 years, including when the grown up Boocock boys spent time at the then-new Keswick Country Club in the late 1940s and early 1950s. It was sold at auction in 1985. On one of her outings, design director Phyllis Koch saw the portrait in McGregor's Antiques in Charlottesville, felt it was the perfect element of authenticity for the hotel, and convinced B.A. to add it to the collection. Norma Flanders was right. The portrait did not come from France.

Lords and Ladies

Within about a year, the word had spread far and wide. In the December 1994 edition of *Andrew Harper's Hideaway Report*, Keswick Hall was named one of its five "U.S. Hideaways of the Year." *Country Inns* magazine also honored it as one of the top inns of 1994. And no wonder. Michael Carlton wrote in *Southern Living* in April of 1995, that "More than 200 years ago, Thomas Jefferson called this slice of Virginia 'America's Eden.' Today it's even better. Keswick Hall is the reason." He called Keswick Hall "a traveler's Eden of uncommon and uncompromising luxury," and elaborated on the stunning views, the "rolling emerald fairways," the breakfast with "oat cakes mounded high with whipped cream and then drizzled with maple syrup," the tennis, and the indoor/outdoor pool. "Of course you can simply retreat to your individually decorated room, sink into hot, scented bathwater, then wrap your body with a pillow-soft bathrobe and go back to bed. Or ask a butler to bring a cup of hot tea to the Drawing Room, where you can sit by the fire and just do nothing. Whatever you decide, you will enjoy this singular hotel. Keswick Hall's service is flawless and unobtrusive, its bedrooms are welcoming and whimsical, and its formal areas exude a surprising informality."

On February 26, 1995, the *Richmond Times-Dispatch* ran a feature article entitled "An English Country Home." It began, "If English lords and ladies existed in Virginia and if they invited guests for the night, the result might be something like Keswick Hall," and described the norms, the decor, the food, and the history of the property. Above all, as Sir Bernard said in the April 1995 issue of *Homes & Gardens*, "What we aim to do with our hotels is offer immaculate, unobtrusive service, comfort, good food, and most importantly, peace. I am obsessive about the need for quiet. People come to rest from the rigours of the modern world, and noise is so stressful."

The lords and ladies in any case would likely have had friends in high places, and Keswick Hall saw its fair share of celebrities throughout the Ashley years, including Anthony Hopkins; Julianne Moore; Gary Oldman; Peter Boyle; director Ridley Scott; Jessica Lange; Ken Burns; Virginia Governor Mark Warner; Virginia Senator John Warner; Joe Biden while he was Senator of Delaware; Sandy Berger, White House advisor to Bill Clinton; Brendan Fraser; Bernard Arnault, richest man in France, on numerous occasions while considering a horse farm in

Mrs. Claudia Lynn, shown here on her Arabian gelding, Tezhal, in the gravel drive in front of Keswick Hall in 1995, strikes as beautiful a pose as any lady on horseback might. (Photo by Winkie Motley.)

Keswick; Carly Fiorina, while running for U.S. Senate in California; Donnatella Versace, and others. In February of 1994, about six months after the grand, soft opening, Buddy Leffers began work as a porter. He naturally interacted with most of the hotel guests, and particularly remembers Fay Wray, Bill Murray, Morgan Freeman, and Paul Newman.

"Fay Wray, one of the leading ladies of King Kong, was here when she was 89 years old, and she was still very attractive. She was staying in Room 21, which looks out over the circle, and I was out there sweeping the gravel. I used to go outside and sweep because after they paved the roads here, they left the front circle gravel, and the gravel used to get carried out to the blacktop, out past the gate. I used to sweep because I thought it looked terrible. Later she came down (I didn't realize she'd been up there on that balcony). She says, 'Young man, was that you out there sweeping?' I said, 'Yes, it was, Miss Wray.' And she said, 'Well, you certainly do know how to handle a broom.' But she was so gracious.

"Bill Murray and his son showed up here without a reservation. I took them up – Bill Murray to Room 9, his son to Room 10. I was getting Mr. Murray settled in. He's a very avid golfer, so he's looking out and said, 'I'd love to play this course.' And I said, 'I'm sorry, Mr. Murray, we can't allow that.' He says, 'What do you mean?' I said, 'We've all seen Caddyshack, sir.' We laughed.

"Morgan Freeman was driven up to the door. I opened the door for him, he shook my hand, deliberately looked at my badge, and said, 'Thank you, Buddy,' just so un-star-like. I just remember how nice he was to go out of his way to do that. I was just a guy who opened a door for him.

"Paul Newman and Joanne Woodward were just delightful, they didn't hide. They were coming and going without any concerns and nobody bothered them. One day I was out on the loading dock and I got paged, and the pagers just let you know they wanted you – they didn't tell you why – so I went ripping in to go upstairs and almost ran over Paul Newman. He was sweating, had an old beat up sweatsuit with nothing special about it and of course his hair was all

All of the public spaces were intended to invite peaceful relaxation, and the drawing room was no exception. The couch came from Sir Bernard Ashley's salon in Brussels, and has since been recovered in deep red, but remains in the same room – now the library, as noted by the distinctive fireplace facade. (Photo by Philip Beaurline.)

This aerial image from the mid-1990s shows the croquet lawn (far left), three tennis courts (background), and the boxwood garden often used for weddings (where the horizon pool is now). Two additional tennis courts and another pool were added in 1997; the horizon pool came in 2003; two more tennis courts came in 2010. (Photo courtesy of Phyllis Koch.)

messed up. So we laughed about the fact that we almost had a collision. Later they were getting ready to go driving and then he looked like Paul Newman would be expected to look. I said, "Mr. Newman, whatever you're doing, keep it up. You look so much better than you did this morning.'"

In April of 1996, Lady Margaret Thatcher was a guest at the hotel while in the area to visit Monticello and receive a statesmanship medal. It was not the only time she came to visit. Dan Abrashoff, front desk manager from 1996-2001, remembers that "she was Chancellor at [The College of] William and Mary and when she was there, B.A. would send his helicopter over to Williamsburg to pick her up and bring her to Keswick. On the occasion of the Thatcher's wedding anniversary, Keswick Hall gave them a set of Virginia Pewter candlesticks."

"B.A. did not like bars," recalled club member Peggy Augustus. "But if you want to have a successful club, you have to have a nice bar that everybody wants to go to." He finally agreed to one in the clubhouse that, not surprisingly, was made to resemble an English pub. (Photo by Philip Beaurline.)

Keswick Club in the 1990s

The *Daily Progress* reported on May 14, 1995, that nearly 300 club memberships had been sold, another sign that all was well at Keswick. B.A. admitted in the article, however, that "Profit projections are not on line as they should be. We are breaking even, just." On June 29, the newspaper stated that the Keswick Estate won approval from the County Board of Supervisors for a $1.3 million expansion of its upscale development, which should have been another good sign. But on September 28, it called the development a "financial sinkhole," and reported that Ashley had filed an $83 million lawsuit against the consulting firm that he said "duped him ... [into making] the deal without their seeking expert advice on the commercial viability of the project and by withholding information that would have shown the deal to be risky." The article also recalled images of the past and reminded readers of the ten different owners since 1947: "Ashley's enterprises represent the latest of many attempts to profit from the Keswick property."

Nevertheless, a July 1996 *Keswick Life* article by Barclay Rives suggested that "bad press" aside, nothing was "amiss" at Keswick. To those who had been club members in the early days, much remained: the graceful lines of the Villa Crawford, the sweeping, glorious countryside, the baying of the restless hounds in the distance, ready for the hunt. There was still plenty of golfing, plenty of tennis. A golf tournament was held every year to benefit Little Keswick School, and in July of 1996, "Tee to Tea" was held at the hotel to benefit the local Red Cross chapter. Supporters could pay either $150 for lunch, golf and an hors d'oeuvres buffet, or $50 for high tea followed by a hotel tour. Nancy Holt, the club's tennis pro since 1992, recalled when tennis star Stan Smith came to Keswick in the mid 1990s to talk to the UVA tennis team. "He ended up doing an exhibition at Keswick Club with me and two other players, set up through Sheridan Snyder, one of our members, who has been involved with UVA Tennis since he played for UVA, graduated in 1958 and later donated the money for a new tennis complex at the university. Being able to play with Stan Smith was an honor and a pleasure." Snyder has great admiration for what Ashley did: "It's a British resort thrown into central Virginia, built with quality and the concept of leisure. Sir Bernard went for quality first."

Shown here in its original blue, the member's lounge in the clubhouse has served as one of the best rooms for small private parties and meetings, bridge and "open cards" groups, book clubs, etc. It also has a perfect view of the golf course. (Photo by Philip Beaurline.)

The initial study of local demographics had indicated that the new Keswick Club had a highly affluent member base not necessarily interested in a family club, thus the high membership fees and the policies that restricted children. But Ashley's commitment to the property included continually revisiting established notions and taking actions designed for the long term good of the whole community. These actions included construction of what was first called the "Hideaway" (and later the Pavilion, now the Tennis & Aquatic Center) with an extra pool and two new hard tennis courts, which opened in 1997, and ever-improving programs to better accommodate families of club members. "Total Fun this Summer" was one such program. It wasn't just "this summer" – it was every summer beginning in the mid 1990s, and it was great. Nancy Holt and Mark Marshall, golf pro until April of 1999 when Eric McGraw took the position, put together Junior Day Camps with professional tennis and golf instruction, swimming lessons, games, activities, and lunch.

The Leader of the Team

By 1997, Keswick Club's membership had topped 530, and Keswick Hall had not only been honored as one of the top 50 inns in the nation by the Zagat Survey, it was also featured on a CBS-TV news segment on "Great Getaways." That same spring, B.A.'s lawsuit was settled out of court for an undisclosed amount, and the media continued to tout Keswick as the place to be. *The Washington Post* on May 17, 1997, called it "A Virginia Community Fit for an English Lord." The Ashley House Spring/Summer 1997 newsletter included an invitation to business travelers as well. Sir Bernard wrote: "I know the life of a businessman. I have endured my share of business meetings. I have observed firsthand how dedicated rest and recreation can energize the imagination and build team spirit.... A business group needs a getaway. It's a tricky balance: the most up-to-date support system, yet a setting so quietly removed that everyday cares drop away, and you can really get down to the heart of business."

Sir Bernard Ashley wanted business travelers to be able to "really get down to the heart of business," in "a setting so quietly removed that everyday cares drop away." John Keating wrote in The Washington Golf Monthly, *October 1996, "Make no mistake about it. Keswick Hall offers the ultimate in pleasure." (Photo by Philip Beaurline.)*

That summer, one business getaway gave everyone an unanticipated image of teamwork. In late August, Hurricane Fran, a storm of such intensity that it caused the highest tide in Virginia since Hurricane Hazel of 1954, rather interfered with Keswick Hall's attempt to host the product launch for all the new Lexus cars. The company had arranged for exclusive use of the hotel for 10 days, and had erected large white tents on the lawn outside the lower level to protect the very expensive automobiles. Abrashoff said, "Needless to say, hurricane force winds with tents was a no go. Peter McDonough scrambled to put what cars he could in his covered area. We brought down the tents, we lost power to the estate, we asked home owners if we could park these cars in their garages to protect them. Talk about a TEAM effort! There were rivers on the golf course." One can only imagine the subsequent work of the grounds crew and head gardener Sue

Dickson to restore the golf course and hotel gardens to their usual splendor.

The leader of the team was unquestionably Sir Bernard himself. Many guests and club members remember his frequent presence around the hotel. He came to lavish, black tie affairs such as the Montpelier Ball, held every November in the hall, wearing a red velvet smoking jacket; he sometimes walked around in a plaid shirt and galoshes overseeing, commenting, and hobnobbing; he took a brief golf lesson with Arnold Palmer, but much preferred flying planes and helicopters with him. "That's where they hit it off," according to Peter McDonough. B.A. also enjoyed Room 1 particularly – it was connected at that time to a study just off the great hall (since removed), and there he was often seen, quietly reading. Sometimes he enjoyed the company of one of his grown sons or daughters, who might also be visiting the hotel. Sometimes he would sit in the Villa reminiscing with staff members about his life and adventures in a truly genuine way.

B.A. also had a lot of fun with the staff. It was known that some of the artwork and furnishings at Keswick Hall came from his European estates. One painting came with a story, related by Dan Abrashoff: "B.A. had a wicked sense of humor and he knew how gullible I was. There was a painting outside Rooms 2 and 3 called 'The Card Sharks.' He told me to keep in confidence that it was the

One of the many English country house touches familiar to guests of Keswick Hall was this display of boots and shoes, in earlier years located under 'The Card Sharks' painting in the south gallery of the first floor.

original done by Caravaggio, and that it was lost for several hundred years but he found it and wanted this priceless artwork hung in Keswick Hall. I, of course, bought into it. We used to give tours of the hall and we would tell people that this was B.A.'s priceless painting, how he found it, etc. – not keeping the promise. After I left Keswick Hall and moved to Texas, I was at the Kimball Art Museum in Ft. Worth with my wife. I turned the corner in this exhibit, and there in front of me is THE original 'Card Sharks' by Caravaggio. It was lost, so that part is correct, but we didn't have the original at Keswick Hall and B.A. was laughing somewhere at the gullible American."

Christmas at Keswick Hall

The Christmas holidays were always a time of extraordinary loveliness at the hotel. Snow blanketed the grounds some years, and inside there were lovely decorations, a gingerbread village in the great hall, and caroling on Christmas Eve. The December 1995 issue of *Homes & Gardens* called Keswick Hall "an ideal setting in which to experience a Colonial-style approach to the festive season," and described how its decorations reflected that style, with wreaths, for example, "brightened by fresh fruit such as apples, cranberries, red- and yellow-skinned pears, and pine cones." The dinner menu may have included the traditional fowl, fish, and pudding at a grand feast such as one would expect at an English estate, but the hall decorations, often done by Dan Patterson of Crozet, were decidedly Virginian and included magnolia and boxwood garlands. One year, taking the hotel's decorating theme to the max, all the tree ornaments were made from Laura Ashley fabrics.

In 1998 a special event was designed to incorporate the traditional aspects of the holiday for anyone interested in a seven-day regional tour based primarily at the hotel. Called "Christmas Day at Keswick Hall" and presented by the National Trust for Historic Preservation, the program began in Washington, D.C. and featured many historic Virginia landmarks including the beautiful Grace Episcopal Church in Keswick. The Grace Church was originally built in 1745, one of six churches founded in Virginia before it was part of a new nation. "We love the quaint church, traditional carols, and hunt country ambiance," said Catherine Cates, who has been coming to Keswick Hall with her family for Christmas since the hotel opened in 1993. The Cates remember "in the early years" when the church had a living nativity with live animals on Christmas

Holidays at Keswick Hall were always special and a little different year to year. One year all the tree ornaments (inset) were made from Laura Ashley fabrics. Many times, fresh fruits, pine cones, and Colonial style decorations reflecting local traditions brightened up the mantles and tabletops. (Ornaments courtesy of Dan Abrashoff; lower photo courtesy of Philip Beaurline.)

Eve, including one very placid donkey that stands out in their memories.

No wonder that *Condé Nast Traveler* magazine ranked Keswick Hall as the #8 small hotel in the world that year. In a November 30, 1998, article entitled "Keswick villa seeing stability," the *Charlottesville Daily Progress* quoted Stephen Beaumont, general manager, affirming the reason: "The difference is made by the people.... it is the best possible service here."

What Sir Bernard Had in Mind

Into 1999, gourmet dinners, murder mystery weekends, literary luncheons, and "the best possible service" continued. But behind the scenes, B.A. had begun exploring options to sell the property. As early as 1997, he had tried to sell "169 acres of unimproved land and 38 empty-but-buildable lots," according to the *C-ville Weekly* in its November 4-10, 1997, edition, but this deal never went through. On May 8, 1999, it was announced in the *Daily Progress* that Ashley had sold the entire property to Orient-Express Hotels, Inc. for $13.5 million. Liz Ratcliffe said in the article that the move was altogether personal for B.A., "part of his planned retirement from the American hotel business." The deal was far from profitable for Ashley, but his impact is undeniable.

The utter transformation of the run-down Villa Crawford into a world-class luxury hotel – incorporating the old, celebrating the new, and always working toward an even better future – must certainly be credited to Sir Bernard Ashley. Lois Perschetz said it best in the *Baltimore* magazine following her visit in April 1995: "We've slept when we wanted, eaten when we wanted, dressed how we wanted, had

This image of the Villa Crawford, showing the Laura Ashley style in its full glory, epitomizes both the elegance and the comfort of the hotel. An early hotel fact sheet called the "Crawford Lounge...an ideal place for afternoon tea, cocktails, or just as a sitting room." (Photo by Philip Beaurline.)

all our needs impeccably met by a caring staff: It's just what Sir Bernard had in mind when he brought the British country-house concept to America. We leave with only one regret – that [he] isn't here for us to thank."

At the 5-year anniversary of the hotel, staff gathered for a photo (newsletter, right). Stephen Beaumont, general manager, remarked, "I believe our achievements are best measured by the thick file of letters I have received from guests, for whom a stay at Keswick Hall has had an impact on their personal lives – as Sir Bernard Ashley has said, "a calm eye in the storm of the modern world." Lead photographer during this period, Philip Beaurline, recalled one occasion Sir Bernard would have been proud to hear of: "The marketing director at the time, Anne Hooff, had comped me and my wife dinner on Valentine's Day. There had been a terrible ice storm the day before, and the hotel and restaurant were forced to close due to the power outage. The power had come back on but the hotel had not yet reopened, and through some miscommunication nobody knew we had a reservation. Marie and I innocently showed up, announced that we had a 6:30 reservation, and with only a very slight hesitation we were ushered in to enjoy the most personal and private dining experience, by the fireplace alone in the dining room. To me this epitomizes the level of service that Bernard Ashley had brought to Keswick."

KESWICK HALL

Fall 1998/Winter 1999

No. XII

KESWICK HALL *Charlottesville, Virginia*

Anniversaries are times for celebration and reflection, recalling the past and looking toward the future. As Keswick Hall reached its 5th anniversary in August, we celebrate the many achievements born from Sir Bernard Ashley's original vision.

Achievements have been many: recognition and accolades from national publications and consumer surveys for our cuisine, service, the wine list, the golf course and amenities; support of local and national charities; welcoming individuals and groups from around the

CELEBRATE

Staff Members of Keswick Hall

world including many celebrities; extending guest facilities with the addition of the Pavilion in 1997; a world wide presence on the internet.

None of these things would have happened, however, were it not for our unusually dedicated staff who are so committed to providing the very best experience for guests. As General Manager, I believe that our achievements are best measured by the thick file of letters that I have received from guests, for whom a stay at Keswick Hall has had an impact on their personal lives—as Sir Bernard Ashley has said, "a calm eye in the storm of the modern world."

We thank the thousands of guests who have visited Keswick Hall over the last five years. You will see in the following pages that as we approach the new millennium, we are continu-ing with innovative new ideas and developments while maintaining the traditions of the past five years. Look for an exciting interactive CD-ROM in the next few months. Join us for a murder mystery weekend. Enjoy our famous Sunday brunch or our equally popular (and extraordinary value!) Sunday evening Jazz series. We look forward to another successful five years, the dawn of a new millennium, but most importantly to your next visit to Keswick Hall.

Stephen Beaumont

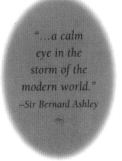

"...a calm eye in the storm of the modern world."
–Sir Bernard Ashley

115

Chapter 6

A Gem in the Heart of Virginia

Keswick Hall, situated in the heart of Virginia among significant historical sites, thoroughbred horse farms, and flourishing wineries, had established itself in the 1990s as a full-fledged, gorgeous, award-winning hotel with a personal touch that kept guests coming back for more. The property's intriguing, patchwork history as both a private home and a country club was largely obscured by the outstanding gardens, furnishings, cuisine, amenities, recreational facilities, and staff that defined and supported its appeal. When Sir Bernard Ashley decided to halt his expansion into historic U.S. properties and was considering various suitors, he looked to Orient-Express for very good reason. Dean Andrews, vice president of North America at that time with Orient-Express, traveled in the fall of 1998 to Sir Bernard's country estate in Provence, France, to negotiate the deal with him and remembers the conversation well: "He turned to me and said, 'You know why I'm going to sell it to you? It is much more than the money – it's most important to me that the hotel be handed over to the right individuals.' He didn't want a trophy buyer. He truly believed Orient-Express could deliver a future for the property." On May 6, 1999, the company that had revived an historic rail line in the early 1980s announced that it was "continuing its rapid expansion in luxury hotels around the world." The then-president of Orient-Express Hotels Ltd., Simon Sherwood, said in the press release, "Those with an appreciation of U.S. history will enjoy the rich Southern tradition and the opportunity to visit many historic landmarks close by, which embody the fabric of America's heritage."

Night or day, the first impression of Keswick Hall is of elegance and grandeur, yet at the same time, guests enjoy a comfortable and at-home feeling. The hotel, purchased by Orient-Express in 1999 from Sir Bernard Ashley, offers this subtle and appealing duality that both sets guests at ease and serves them with the highest standards. (Photo by Joe Vaughn.)

The very first "Express d'Orient" that left Paris for Vienna in 1883 was part of a long distance passenger train service renamed "Orient Express" in 1891 (operating separately from the Orient-Express of today). Over the years, as it ran regularly between Paris and Istanbul, numerous associations in literature and other media created and cemented an image of intrigue and elegance. Beginning with a reference to the train in Bram Stoker's 1897 *Dracula*, and followed by Agatha Christie's famous 1934 *Murder on the Orient Express*, what began as a simple international rail line turned legendary. In times past called "the train of kings and the king of trains," Orient Express became an iconic symbol of exciting, luxurious adventure, but many of the cars fell into disrepair when more high-speed travel began to predominate in Europe. In 1977 James B. Sherwood decided to resurrect some of the original sleeper, restaurant, and Pullman carriages from the early 20th century as part of a venture to expand his own successful company into the luxury travel business. He spent millions over the next five years to purchase 35 of the old cars and restore them to their original splendor. On May 25, 1982, with champagne and fanfare, Sherwood christened the renewed London to Venice voyage of this fabulous train dubbed *Venice Simplon-Orient-Express*. His company had also purchased the Hotel Cipriani in Venice in 1976, giving the unique train a perfect destination.

The hallmark of Orient-Express has been to create and manage extraordinary travel experiences, and the 1999 purchase of Keswick Hall in the heart of Virginia provided another outstanding opportunity. By this time the Villa Crawford and its hundreds of acres, despite

The hotels, trains, and cruises of Orient-Express provide luxurious and extraordinary travel experiences all over the world. Shown here are the Andean Explorer and Urcos Bridge on Peru Rail in South America and the Observation Car on the Eastern & Orient Express in southeast Asia. (Peru photo by Eduardo Saldarriaga; E&O photo by Willy Tang.)

KESWICK HALL
AT MONTICELLO

numerous owners, uses, and conversions, had been part of the local landscape for nearly a century. It had inspired dreams and doubts, both in good measure, and had proven itself a keeper. Orient-Express had its hands on a gem and knew it. Naturally, enthusiasm abounded from the get-go.

One goal, moving into the new millennium, was to preserve and protect the property's authenticity and natural surroundings. The new logo – Keswick Hall at Monticello – affirmed an association not only with Thomas Jefferson's estate nearby, but also with historic integrity in general. Important as well, and commended by all, was a commitment to the environment evidenced by the goal of Audubon certification for the golf course.

Looking Ahead

Another goal was to find ways to enhance the unique guest experience by improving or adding to almost all the interior and exterior spaces, including but not limited to: more than doubling the number of guest rooms, adding a new restaurant and bar, ensuring state of the art conference rooms, installing an additional outdoor pool, and building a spa and an exercise room at the club. According to the December 1999 issue of *Keswick Life*, the company intended make sure that the plans would "keep the feeling of Virginia in the enhancement of Keswick."

In this same issue, and again in the *Daily Progress* on June 16, 2000, a specific expansion plan including 75 additional guest rooms was announced. The County Board of Supervisors "OK'd" the plans, according to a *Daily Progress* article on October 19, 2000, and gave an initial thumbs-up for a new wing and ten new two- and four-unit guest villas with their own gardens and pool. The expansion would bring the total number of guest rooms to 123. Nays and yays weighed in from those seeing huge challenges and those wanting to meet them head on. Longstanding concerns about development and natural resources were voiced by some local residents, countered by assurances that everything would be done to protect long term viability.

In the end, the same 48 guest rooms that Sir Bernard Ashley had set up are the

Taken during the gentle Virginia autumn from an upper floor guest room, this view looks at the golf course toward the east, a familiar sight for anyone who has visited Keswick Hall. Many a gorgeous sunrise has also been enjoyed from this vantage point. (Photo by Joe Vaughn.)

ones that remain today. Instead of expanding the size of the hotel, Orient-Express chose to focus on other areas, such as encouraging more local guests to come and discover the property. Any number of sources had indicated that when Keswick Club opened with full media coverage as a private club in 1992, the community had gotten the impression that the whole property – Keswick Hall, Club & Estate – was private. To begin undoing the rather fixed image, it was decided to remove the manned front (west) gate that stood at the entrance near the tennis courts, and replace it with card-reading technology several hundred feet farther in. As noted in the March 21, 2001, *Daily Progress*, management considered this gate to be a deterrent to visitors, and homeowners considered it a safety feature. A compromise was soon reached involving a round-the-clock security team stationed at the east gate, and a keypad and intercom system for residents and visitors at the

Keswick Schematic Design...........

The plan to expand Keswick Hall by adding 75 new guest rooms did not come to pass. Orient-Express explored the idea, then chose to focus on other areas of growth, such as the new restaurant, Fossett's. (Image courtesy of Winkie Motley, Keswick Life, *December 1999.)*

Wildlife on Keswick's golf course and hiking trails is not uncommon. White-tailed deer such as these are often seen, seemingly watching and waiting for something interesting to happen. (Photo courtesy of Amy Lewis.)

newly placed west gate.

Members of Keswick Club – both those who own one of the beautiful homes on the estate and those who live in the local community and beyond – have successfully navigated their unique situation for years. They recognize the mutually beneficial relationship they have with hotel guests, evident on the balance sheet as well as on the property every day. Immaculately maintained grounds and facilities are available to both (to club members all the time, and to hotel guests for the duration of their stay). Specialized golf, tennis and fitness instruction continue to be as top rate as the facilities, to say nothing of holiday parties, fly fishing, balloon rides, clay shooting excursions, cooking schools, walking with the hounds, wine tastings, croquet, archery, bridge, hiking trails, history tours, garden tours, children's activities, and more.

From a hotel guest's perspective, the transition to Orient-Express ownership was seamless. For Michael McCarthy, who wrote about his visit to Keswick Hall in the summer of 2002 for the *Washington Flyer*, a magazine and travel guide, "exclusive" apparently still meshed with "laid-back and comfortable." He noted "Old World character"…"hunt country allure"… and "a timeless sense of style" in his article, and went on to paint an enchanting picture with words: "Keswick is like visiting your rich uncle's place. It has the trappings of grandeur, but the charm and warmth of a Southern family reunion…But we don't spend a lot of time indoors. During the day, we hike the shaded paths that wind through the property. With miles of dense green landscape surrounding us, isolation has never felt so perfect. At night, we retreat to a patio outside of our room. The air is cool and a cloudy night paints the entire valley black. A breeze from over the ridge eventually hustles away the clouds, revealing an orange moon that climbs the horizon and a swirl of stars against the chalkboard sky. I want this rich uncle to invite us back again and again."

The dense green landscape surrounding Keswick Hall has enticed many guests to return again and again. (Photo by Joe Vaughn.)

Audubon Certification for the Golf Course

That dense green landscape got its own measure of satisfaction a few months later. In 1999 Orient-Express had given Peter McDonough, Keswick's longstanding golf course superintendent, a priority – he was to lead a lengthy process toward the course's designation as a "Certified Audubon Cooperative Sanctuary." The certification, received on December 17, 2002, and maintained since then, confirmed Audubon International's recognition of the high degree of environmental planning and stewardship involved in the construction and maintenance of the course. At that time, of more than 16,000 golf courses nationwide, only 371 had been so awarded, and only six of those in Virginia. Peter Bronski, an Audubon staff ecologist, said in a lengthy *Daily Progress* article on July 13, 2003, that McDonough exceeded the minimum requirements of the certification program "in all categories."

Arnold Palmer's group got involved in the Audubon project as well, not only in lengthening the course by some 400 yards, but also in "naturalizing" 25 acres and reconstructing some elements of the course "with an eye toward maintaining [its] serenity." This work mirrored McDonough's belief that "golf courses have to be recognized as recreational vehicles and also cohabitate with the natural surroundings and the environment." Allowing some areas of the course to revert to their natural state, significantly reducing pesticide usage, saving several million gallons of water per year, and making golfers aware of the increased wildlife habitat all went a long way toward McDonough's goal of "raising the bar of environmental awareness." One challenge was met creatively – with a new dog. Wendy, Keswick's happy border collie, chases geese off the course over to the lake, where their droppings are not so bothersome. She is so much a part of the staff that her photo joins the rest of the longstanding golf course maintenance crew on the hotel's employee photo wall.

Reworking the golf course for Audubon certification, attained in 2002, made the course more environmentally friendly, but not easier. Shown here is the 5th hole, a long par 4 with a very difficult tee shot over wetlands. The narrow fairway is guarded by a stream all the way down the right hand side, with the approach shot into a two-tiered green. (Photo courtesy of Peter McDonough.)

A common sight around the property: Wendy the Border Collie en route with Peter McDonough to her favorite stomping grounds, the golf course, where she happily chases the geese away.

Wispy drifts float upward off the pool (right) just as morning mist settles into the recesses of terrain on the golf course beyond, with its ever-different, glorious sunrises (left). Sometimes even in winter, a swimmer enjoys leisurely laps in the hotel's serenity pool. (Photo on right courtesy of Anthony Glover; photo on left by Joe Vaughn; photo above courtesy of Catherine Cates.)

A Peaceful New Pool

The enhancements to the golf course were not created especially for those enjoying the view from the new million-dollar horizon pool (or infinity edge pool, or illusion pool, or serenity pool – as you will). But one might think so when reading Ruth Hart's impressions in her *Albemarle* magazine article in the summer of 2003. She discusses the illusion that the "glassine surface" of the pool creates

"in combination with the sound of falling water.... the eye is drawn, rather nearly launched off the disappearing edges into a timeless landscape. The muted, hazy light of an early summer morning cast over rolling hills, and shades of color ranging from sage to dark evergreen might leave the viewer wondering where this enchanting place is...."

The 63' x 36' pool, heated for use in all but the coldest months, replaced a lovely boxwood garden with a new kind of beauty – soft, wispy mist drifts upward from the water's surface in the cooler, early morning hours, a spectacular image often coupled, at the same time of day, with similar pockets of mist in the random recesses of terrain on the golf course. Somewhat later in the morning, this pool has often been the site of a solitary swimmer doing leisurely laps even before the housekeepers, as a quiet, graceful, unobtrusive team, bring the fresh, white towels and chair covers and prepare the area for the day ahead. Hotel guests and club members have been delighted to discover not only the special moments, the views, the serenity, and the refreshing water, but also a few surprises. Underwater speakers deliver unexpected music to those who choose to swim, and in the cool shade above ground, talented spa therapists offer delightful "poolside pampering treatments" such as chair massage and reflexology.

Fossett's

Naturally, whether guests hike, golf, swim, or luxuriate in the sun, they enjoy an excellent meal. Long gone are the 1950s Chicken Salad Sandwiches and the Plantation Buttermilk Pie that had been available in the lower level 19th Hole tavern of country club days. Even the very fine cuisine of the first ten years of Keswick Hall's era as a grand hotel received a complete make-over with the addition of its fine dining restaurant, Fossett's, which had first been mentioned in the May 12-18, 1999, *Charlottesville Observer*. In the article, Dean Andrews, director of operations, called it "the biggest change" Orient-Express would make: "a freestanding restaurant with a concept behind it." The most obvious change was the restaurant's location: up one level to the first floor overlooking the golf course, or as Andrews later put it, "up to the view."

Fossett's opened about a year after the horizon pool went in. An article in the *Daily Progress* on June 23, 2004, noted that the hotel was still sometimes associated with "stuffiness," a situation the restaurant would hopefully rectify. Management had made a serious study of what would make sense not only for Keswick Hall's guests, but also for the community at large. The article suggested a second look. "The Hall has rolled out the welcome mat, and with it, a message: Forget what you've heard and judge for yourself." Designed to be "elegant yet relaxed, so it could be a favourite among locals, but also a destination restaurant of visitors to the area," noted Michael Pownall, general manager at the time, "Fossett's is perfectly positioned to offer gourmets an exciting culinary getaway in the heart of the Monticello wine

To better take in the spectacular view of the golf course and to open up a great deal of space on the terrace level for private functions, the hotel's restaurant was moved up one level. In June of 2004, award-winning Fossett's opened its doors.

region." This approachability, combined with a prime location within the hotel and great menu and service options, all gave Fossett's a highly competitive edge.

As it turned out, the floor-to-ceiling windows enclosing Fossett's provided an exceptional vista. Guest Pamela Thibault said in the *Daily Progress* article, "I love the simplicity. The real art is the view." Fossett's fireplace, which had previously been a unique gathering place on cooler evenings on the outdoor terrace during the Ashley years, became interior instead and is lit every night throughout the cooler months to provide a charming ambiance, and the outside darkness of the winter months is illuminated by the abundant stars of the Virginia countryside, some well placed exterior lights, and, winter or summer, the occasional spectacular lightning storm. In the warmer months, fireworks associated with wedding receptions and the 4th of July are perfectly orchestrated and fill the expanse of sky with a fabulous light show that no one wants to miss.

The construction of Fossett's allowed many possibilities for weddings, holiday events, and special parties on the lower level. Tents such as this expand the space to accommodate groups up to 400. Keswick's talented culinary staff prepares not only course after amazing course for Fossett's guests, but also simultaneously for those attending private events, bringing themselves both repeat accolades and repeat guests. (Photo courtesy of Jen Fariello.)

Fossett's took its name from Thomas Jefferson's head cook, Edith Fossett, whose likeness graces the dining room and whose legacy is seen in a culinary stamp that creatively incorporates fresh, local fare into a French foundation. Jefferson spent nearly all of his 16 years of retirement at Monticello, and in its simple kitchen, Edith Fossett developed her own unique culinary style after having trained at the White House under French chef Honoré Julian. Edith creatively used produce from Monticello's extensive gardens (of peas alone, it is said there were 19 different kinds planted at Monticello) along with local dairy products and Virginia's abundant fish and game. Daniel Webster, a contemporary of Thomas Jefferson and, some would say, the creator of the American lexicon, who visited Monticello in 1824, noted that "dinner is served in half Virginian, half French style, in good taste and abundance." Dinner guests of the 21st century express themselves differently. Rave reviews of Fossett's led to its participation in local restaurant events such as Restaurant Week, when many of the best establishments in the local area offer a sampling of their menus at a special price. In July of 2010, one reviewer wrote: "So yum doesn't even begin to describe how good the menu is at Fossett's during Restaurant Week!"

Edith's style has been interpreted in various ways. John Brand, Fossett's first executive chef, began his career washing dishes. "He was a self made chef," recalled Scott Meynig, the hotel's food and beverage director who began his own tenure at Keswick as a front server on Fossett's opening day and has since been an integral part of its operation. "Whenever he spoke in a cooking class or to a group of guests about food, he would always start out by saying that he did not go to a culinary school. He was a very good kitchen manager and brought with him a raft of recipes and talent that put Fossett's on the map, including *Esquire* magazine's "Best Restaurants of 2004.'" Chef Brand said in the *Daily Progress* on June 22, 2004, that his cuisine "instinctively tastes good." His menu had five sections – First, Second, Farm, Harvest, and Dessert – as well as a five-course tasting menu, available with or without wine pairings, all of which left "room for fun" as he put it. Guests may remember the red pear carpaccio, Virginia jumbo lump crab with mango vanilla relish, steelhead trout with balsamic braised beef

Hand in hand with the opening of Fossett's came an outstanding option for very special occasions: "Signature Tables," set for small parties either on the ellipse of the pool or in the library as shown. Guests can request an evening of private, elegant dining featuring a special, superbly set, candlelit table, a designated server, and a specially prepared menu. The library of the Villa Crawford provides a romantic setting for a happy couple or, as in this photo, an equally warm setting for a small family gathering. (Photo courtesy of Jen Fariello.)

Mainstays

These classic, simple but elegant dishes
have been the mainstay of superb dining for ages.

COLD WATER LOBSTER COCKTAIL
Sauce ravigote
14

CREAMY ORGANIC CAULIFLOWER SOUP
Beautiful winter soup of fresh organic
cauliflower, gruyere gougere
7

ROASTED HERBED LAMB
Roasted rack of herb-cured lamb,
pomme purée, winter vegetables bouquetiere,
Hunter sauce
38

SAUTÉED ROCKFISH
Sautéed Virginia rockfish filet, grilled baby
asparagus, pommes dauphine, crab sauce
34

CLASSIC ICED
GRAND MARNIER SOUFFLE
Ice cold Grand Marnier soufflé,
candied orange and almond sablé
9

Thomas Jefferson *TJ's Power*

Visitors to Mr. Jefferson's home called
his cuisine half Virginian, half French.

RAVIOLI OF BRAISED LAMB SHOULDER
Beet puree, creamed leeks and
parsnip chips, natural jus
12

OYSTERS AND SWEETBREADS
Potato hay and micro watercress salad,
Red Cloud potato chowder with Kite's bacon
14

MONTICELLO COW PEAS CASSOULET
Smoked onions, wild mushrooms,
pear tomatoes and wild garlic, wilted winter kale
24

GRYFFON'S AERIE BEEF BOUILLE
AND GRILLED TENDERLOIN
Root vegetables persillade and grilled pears,
Sauce au poivre
35

VIRGINIA GENTLEMAN'S CAKE
Peanut-caramel ice cream,
Valhrona fondue
9

Edith Fossett *She of the kitchen*

This menu highlights the amazing influence that
Edith Fossett had on Jefferson's cuisine.

SOUTHERN FRIED QUAIL
Vidalia onion – apple jam, grilled Johnny Cake
and truffle fried quail egg
10

A TRIO OF PED FARM'S LETTUCES
Salad with winter root vegetables and alliums,
Surrey County peanuts vinaigrette
8

SLOW COOKED PAN DUCK
Spoon bread, green tomato compote, wilted slaw
with three cabbages, cracked mustard duck glace
30

VIRGINIA PORK TASTING
Grapevine smoked pork tenderloin, orange
braised pork belly, braised winter greens, good
luck beans, glazed chestnuts, Trotter bordelaise
28

SWEET POTATO PIE
Vanilla ice cream laced with Nicely's Honey,
pecan praline and paw paw conserve
9

Exploration

Thomas Jefferson would surely have celebrated
the adventurous nature of this menu.

FAUX GRAS TORCHON
Truffle explosion with brioche crisp
11

VIRTUAL SUMMER
Tomato cloud, basil gelee,
fresh mozzarella-fig balsamic balloon
10

KING SALMON "SOUS VIDE"
Grated salt-cured salmon on olive oil potato,
baby vegetables and mushroom bacon,
black grape emulsion
32

DESSERT TASTING
Molten-powder gelee
9

Introduced in 2009, this themed menu brought new accolades to Fossett's. It has undergone various and numerous changes since then, evolving constantly, sometimes daily, depending in part on the season and the availability of local products. Fossett's chefs have a seemingly endless ability to elicit high praise. (Menu design by Sara Augustine.)

shortribs, and Chateaubriand with black truffle parmesan potatoes.

Chef Craig Hartman, who wore the executive chef's hat for several years beginning in 2007, increased the use of local, heritage products farmed sustainably such as eggs and chicken from Polyface Farm and beef from Gryffon's Aerie, as well as produce from Keswick's own extensive herb and vegetable garden. Chef Hartman brought, according to Meynig, "the perfect marriage of local ingredients, modern techniques, a culinary connection to the food- and wine-loving Mr. Jefferson, and his own personal charm. He could describe anything edible in such a lyrical way that you would want it *now*." In 2009 Chef Hartman introduced a new and well received menu format with four themes: Mainstays (classic, simple, and elegant), Edith Fossett ("She of the kitchen," highlighting her amazing influence on Jefferson's cuisine), Thomas Jefferson (the classic half-French, half-Virginian), and Exploration ("a culinary adventure that TJ himself would have celebrated"). His brunch menu included his family's recipe for sweet potato biscuits and an all-time guest favorite, "sticky love bacon" – baked with garlic and brown sugar and as scrumptious as it sounds.

In Fossett's kitchen in 2009, Chef Hartman prepares one of his specialties. More and more, the culinary staff uses local, heritage products. (Photo by Joe Vaughn.)

After Chef Hartman left to open his own very successful "BarBQ Exchange" in Gordonsville, Dean Maupin took the reins. Maupin had been featured in the hotel's spring/summer 2005 newsletter when, as Chef de Cuisine under Chef Brand, he enjoyed creating signature items by what he called "cooking off the cuff – showcasing the best products we can find at any particular moment," an idea that defined Fossett's more and more as time went on. After becoming executive chef in 2010, Maupin almost immediately won a "Rising Star" award at a gala Washington, D.C., event, where he served up duck confit and ricotta gnocchi with butternut squash, arugula, cracklin's, and grated Wisconsin SarVecchio parmesan. "His latest menu is about smaller plates that give the diner an opportunity to taste more of his flavor combinations and literally not be so weighed down by them," said Meynig.

The Fossett's experience was beautifully enhanced in the dining room through the spring of 2010 by pianist George Melvin, who played many evenings to the delight of many and is certainly missed. His widow Alfreda said, "His extensive mental repertoire easily exceeded 1000 tunes," including primarily jazz, swing, R&B, and popular tunes from the last half century. George Melvin brought both warmth and excitement to a room with his music, and was able to play almost any song requested. If the title didn't ring a bell for him, all he needed was a few of the opening notes, which the guest gladly (and very softly) provided. He also played regularly in the Villa Crawford, drawing the community to Fossett's bar, which opened in late 2004, and he played for special occasions like Christmas Eve, being the perfect accompaniment to caroling sing-a-longs.

The Villa Crawford

Another way that Keswick Hall encouraged more members of the local community to experience its uniqueness was with its "Villa Lunch," launched in 2006 under the direction of general manager at the time, Anthony McHale. Business groups, couples, and friends are drawn to the excellent five-course spread in the Villa Crawford which, as designed, is centrally located between the main part of the hotel and the pool and club. Guests walking down the grand old staircase in the villa around lunch time are immediately enveloped by inviting aromas and enticed by lovely displays of salads, charcuterie, smoked salmon, steaming entrees and sides, and fresh breads, as well as desserts that one guest called "to die for." In the summertime, the view and the breeze invite terrace dining, and in the winter, the wood-burning fireplaces toast up the snooker room, bar, and library. Actor Robert Duvall and former Vice-President Dick Cheney are among those who have enjoyed the scrumptious bounty of Villa Lunch. Bob Reid, tennis pro at the Keswick Club from 1965-1971, came quite a number of times in his mid-90s to dine with a group of friends in the library. He, like many who spent a good deal of time here in days past and then returned years later, often looked around, smiled, and reflected about the old days and how things used to be.

The library in the Villa Crawford, in its early 20th-century days called the "reception room," is well stocked with books about Virginia or by Virginians due to the efforts of former porter Buddy Leffers and his wife around 2002. A plaque in their honor hangs in the room. Leffers said, "When the renovation was done after Orient-Express took over, the general

George Melvin, Keswick's pianist for about five years, is shown in the Villa Crawford. If only the sound of his music could accompany this image... (Photo courtesy of Alfreda Melvin.)

manager decided that if we were going to have a library, it should be a Virginia library. My wife Ruth and I volunteered to do this. We bought boxes and boxes of books from various sources, labeled everything in all the different categories, and at one point had over 600 books." Just beyond the wooden floors that mark the boundary between the old part of the hotel and the new, just down the hall toward Fossett's, guests can find a glass case with a lovely selection of Jeffersonian reproductions, yet another connector from past to present.

Thomas Jefferson and Wine

In keeping with Thomas Jefferson's norm, superb wine has certainly also been part of the fine dining experience at Keswick Hall. Sommelier Richard Hewitt derives his job description from the original meaning of sommelier: "the one in charge of the King's provisions." At Keswick Hall, he is in charge of all of the wine on the extensive wine list, the production of "Edith's" wine since 2008 which includes custom-crush, private-label Chardonnay, Petit Verdot, and Viognier, and the property's "Courtside Vineyard," planted with Petit Manseng in 2010 and faring beautifully. Hewitt chose the Petit Manseng varietal not only for the flavor of the wine it will make, but also because it has a thick skin and is more resistant to the "nasty" issues grapes can have. It can also hang longer on the vine if need be or if the winemaker chooses to let it, resulting in higher sugar content, that is, a sweeter wine.

Sommelier Richard Hewitt oversees the 5000 or so bottles of wine housed at Keswick Hall, directs the production of its private label Edith's wine, and hopes guests will take the opportunity to participate in various aspects of the wine-making process. (Photo by Joe Vaughn.)

Being sommelier at Keswick Hall has put Richard Hewitt into some very amusing situations. He tells one story this way: "A few years ago there was a Rolling Stones concert at Scott Stadium at UVA. Since each band member required at least five rooms for his entourage, it was impossible for all of the 'Stones' to stay at Keswick. We did house Mick Jagger, his body-guard (a blond brut with a Tweety bird tattoo on both arms), and three young women who were termed his assistants.

"The day after the concert one of the nubile assistants approached the restaurant and asked if

Keswick's private label Edith's Chardonnay debuted in 2008 and was soon followed by Petit Verdot and Viognier. In 2010, Petit Manseng was planted in the property's own "Courtside Vineyard." (Label design by Sara Augustine.)

it would be possible for them to eat in Fossett's that night. It was a busy night and I knew it would cause a disturbance if Mick walked through the dining room. I explained this to the nubile but she countered that they did this all the time and no one ever really noticed them. I finally talked them into coming at 9:30 so that the majority of guests would have departed. They arrived punctually and I escorted them to their table. As soon as they entered Fossett's however, the room became very quiet. Once the group was at their table, I noticed that everyone in the dining room was staring at Jagger. Almost immediately a couple of guests were out of their chairs and approaching the group. The body guard 'Tweety' was outside sitting on the sofa, drinking a 'juicy.'

"I intervened and cut off the eager guests, asking them to please give Jagger et al. a few private moments. The guests said they understood and returned to their tables. There was suddenly a flurry of cell phone activity as almost every guest still in Fossett's pulled out their phones and began to call friends. This was fairly disruptive as well, so we had to ask the guests that insisted on making calls to do so outside the restaurant. This, in turn, emptied out the restaurant as everybody had someone to call to tell them they were dining with Mick Jagger, who was unperturbed through all this and just wanted to talk about Thomas Jefferson and his chef Edith Fossett."

Keswick's Gardens

Unquestionably, the Monticello garden that supplied Edith's kitchen was the inspiration for the one that Keswick's head gardener Amy Lewis planted in 2009 to coincide with the new Fossett's menu celebrating the cuisine of Thomas Jefferson's Monticello days. The vegetables and culinary herbs were chosen "with an emphasis on heirloom varieties," she said. "Heirloom are any open pollinated seed varieties that have been passed down through generations for at least 50 years. We purchased the majority of our heirloom seeds from Monticello. Heirloom are thought to have better flavor, but their appearance often looks distorted."

Many decades ago, in its earliest days, the property had been noted as a place of beauty. The original Villa Crawford was described by a visitor in 1914 as having an "apple orchard, dogwood, wild plum blossoms, honeysuckle, wild violets and iris, tulips and hyacinths in every imaginable hue, little blue daisies ... in a scented riot of color which takes the dormant imagination by storm." References to the adjacent property purchased to add acreage included that it was "famous for its fruits and flowers, which have afforded pleasure and delight to the many who have honored it with a visit."

Curtis Shaver, sous chef, rides a bicycle from the kitchen down to the chef's garden, where he picks the herbs or vegetables needed at the time and loads up his basket for the trip back to the kitchen.

But it is hardly imaginable that the grounds and gardens were, in those early days, even possibly maintained in as beautiful a manner as they have been in recent years. Amy Lewis credits Sue Dickson, who preceded her in the 1990s as head gardener, with preserving much of the old growth that survived the massive renovations, establishing some of the perennial beds that are now very mature, and laying the groundwork for the gardens that delight visitors to this day. Amy and her staff, responsible for the seven acres immediately surrounding the hotel, work year-round to plant, water, feed, weed, pull, divide, re-plant, mow, clip, and trim. They maintain 162 outside planter boxes, 20 beds of annuals, and 11 beds of perennials. They grow many annuals from seed, re-use bulbs for the next season's cut flowers, hang-dry hydrangeas for Christmas tree decorations, train climbing plants up fishing lines, coordinate the colors of

The chef's herb and vegetable garden as it looks in June, already abundant with much produce including beans, tomatoes, beets, and dill. (Photo courtesy of Amy Lewis.)

Keswick's Kwanzan Cherry Trees (Prunus serrulata 'Kwanzan'). Amy Lewis, head gardener, says,"They really do make a great show!" (Photo courtesy of Vladimir Mednikov.)

the flowers and plants in a given area to the surrounding décor, consider color and fragrance and maximum visibility when planning beds, stay ahead of plant enemies like Japanese beetles and aphids, and fill bird feeders. Yara Acker, assistant gardener, maintains a magnificent, continuous display of fresh cut flowers throughout the hotel and club.

The flowering cherry trees, apricot trees, and gorgeous bulbs of spring, the roses and crepe myrtles of summer, the brilliant foliage of the maples and oaks in the fall, and the holly, hellebores, and evergreens of winter – each of these has contributed in good measure to the refreshment and delight of hotel guests and club members alike. Strolling the grounds or hiking the trails to take in all that beauty adds the element of activity, engaging the body and the mind together toward a renewed well being. According to Colette Long, Keswick's health and wellness director, activity and relaxation have a healthy, counterbalancing effect on each other. Since her arrival in 2002, Colette has encouraged guests to recognize the beneficial effects of both. The pampering, indulgent treatments at the spa and the lively, invigorating activities available in the fitness center each have their place, and in fact form a great model for good health: take time to relax and take time to be active. This dual aspect is what Colette loves about her job – she not only gets to do both, she also gets to promote both. She calls it "healing hands in both directions."

"Ah" Moments in the Spa and Fitness for All

The indulgences available at the spa are designed to take the guest "on a journey." The moment a guest enters the meditation room while waiting for treatment, an "ah" moment occurs, with the appealing decor, soft and welcoming atmosphere, and fruit and teas inviting the guest to take that first step toward relaxation. The treatment rooms are larger than most, and Keswick's often-praised therapists provide the exceptional next step. One of Colette's favorite guests is Mrs. Peters, who "loved it here" the first time she visited, " – had the time of her life." The next time Mrs. Peters came, it became apparent how much she had loved the spa services – she spent four full days enjoying one treatment after the next, taking her pick – one by one – of many options: Swedish massage, deep tissue massage, the four-handed "ultimate" massage, hot stone massage, reflexology, or hot poultice massage. One specialty offered at the spa is the "Keswick Reserve": a "vineyard-inspired" treatment that is completely a propos in Virginia wine country. It starts with a red wine greeting and includes massage, body scrub, body mask, facial mask, and face and body smoother – all done with elements of the plant from the grape vine to the seed, and all done to infuse the body with anti-oxidants and anti-aging polyphenois. Mrs. Peters knew a good thing when she found it. So have many others – club members and hotel guests alike.

The apricot trees that produce these glorious blossoms in the spring stand just behind the hydrangeas on the main drive leading to Keswick Hall's entrance. (Photo courtesy of Casey Lockwood.)

On the active side, those who want to take advantage of the beautiful fitness center, opened in 2000, have their pick of many cardio machines, Cybex strength training equipment, and free weights. Group exercise and yoga classes, available on a set schedule, have always been both fun and encouraging. And for ten years, Keswick Club members and staff have participated in an annual 5K

Spa treatments come in many varieties and await guests looking for different kinds of relaxation. (Photo by Philip Beaurline.)

At the hotel's west gate in June of 2010, participants prepared to set off on the 10th annual 5K Run benefiting Hospice of the Piedmont. (Photo courtesy of Colette Long.)

run that benefits the Hospice of the Piedmont – not only a good cause, but also another way to enjoy the company of others while maintaining good fitness levels.

Singing Golf Clubs

Much has changed over time regarding the optimal fitness levels associated with various recreational activities, and golf, one of Keswick's premier activities, is no exception. Keswick's fitness center gives golfers numerous ways to prepare themselves for the challenging course that awaits them. "Yoga and pilates can improve a player's range of motion, and strengthening the back, shoulders and wrists is important, especially if you go at the ball hard," says Eric McGraw, the club's PGA golf professional since the spring of 1999. "If the club's not singing, you ain't a-swinging." He warns players not to assume that the length of Keswick's course reflects its level of difficulty. It's a beautiful course to be sure, with its rolling terrain, mature hardwoods, and mountain views, and the remarkable blend of Fred Findlay's 1949 design and Arnold Palmer's 21st century renovations means the kind of course you walk away from and remember every single hole because they are so different from one another. It's the mere 6,519 yards that fools people – to a golfer that sounds like a short course, but yardage isn't everything.

During McGraw's first summer at Keswick, the TearDrop Tour Championship, a developmental tour for up-and-coming pros and those returning to this level of play, was held on its course. On July 15, 1999, the *Daily Progress* covered this "first professional golf event in the Charlottesville area" where "some 215 golfers will be competing for $200,000 in prize money." One player took a look at the yardage and figured he would tear it apart. Word of his boast, combined with the tournament director's fearless "Make the course as tough as you want" directive, gave McGraw and course superintendent McDonough license to grow the roughs and pack the greens to the nth degree possible. "We grew the rough almost two feet high," said McGraw. "If you missed the fairway, you were lucky to find the ball. The tournament director called me on the last day of the tournament from out on the course, yelled 'Do you hear this noise!?' and held the phone toward a very loud rumbling sound in the background. It was Peter, rolling the greens with the heavy cement rollers to make them harder and faster. The tournament director had suggested to Peter that the course was as difficult as it needed to be, but Peter's Irish blood was running high and there was no stopping that train. Needless to say, no one tore the course up."

The appeal of the Keswick course is not just its deceivingly challenging length and layout. What appealed to McGraw from the start was the club's philosophical approach, which he says is to "honor the game in a classic and traditional manner." Emphasis on the experience, on having a course that players can walk if they want to, on instruction that's tailored to an individual's learning style – these elements set Keswick apart and "grow the game." If you have fun with golf, he suggests, your enthusiasm will get someone else to play, and soon more and more people will be playing. Besides that, there is nothing like four hours of enjoying the company of a friend along with beautiful, panoramic scenery that's gorgeous every season – all while tuning up your swing and shaving a few strokes off your handicap.

Beautiful, panoramic scenery, the company of friends, and Keswick's challenging golf course – what could be better? (Photo courtesy of Jen Fariello.)

Courts for All

A tennis player might counter there is nothing like a well placed drop shot or a forehand drive deep into the alley past your opponent on lighted courts while the moon is rising over the trees to the east. But at Keswick there is plenty of room for all, especially since two new tennis courts were added in October 2010. The frequent use of the other five courts during scheduled matches and tournaments had affirmed the need for more, said Nancy Holt, USPTA tennis pro. She has been organizing matches and providing lessons since the Ashley years, always encouraging players to remember the basics like good preparation and footwork, and she was tremendously pleased to be able to have the new, extra set of courts for club members and hotel guests to play on while the other courts are being used. The new courts are a "hydrocourt" design that has a sub-surface watering

Tennis at Keswick has opportunities for both fun and community service. Participants in the 2008 7th annual "In the Pink" tournament (right, above) play to benefit "Marianne's Room" at the Martha Jefferson Hospital, a cancer patient support and resource center. On another, equally gorgeous summer afternoon, Jessica Olingy (right) practiced overheads to improve her game. Beginning in 2010, tennis players could also choose to play on the two new "hydrocourts" that were installed. (Photo, right, by Josh Gibson.)

138

system but plays like a standard clay or "har-tru" surface, which is said to be easier on the knees and slows down the pace of the ball to allow more preparation time.

The credit for the new hydrocourts, as Nancy Holt proudly pointed out during the 2010 ribbon-cutting ceremony, belonged to Cary Brent, who has been "building the value of the property," as he says, since the early Ashley years. Other capital improvement projects he has spearheaded and guided include "Phase II" of Keswick Estates (the development beginning in 2005 of 167 acres of the property into 48 additional home sites, every one lovely, exclusive, and serene), 2010's "Courtside Vineyard," and 2011's private dining wine cellar, "Treble." The wine cellar was designed not only to house the 5000+ bottles available to discerning guests, but also to be a unique venue for wine tastings or private parties with a dedicated waitstaff. Its decor alone, its solid wood and stone recesses, invite an experience that guests do not soon forget – a goal in keeping with that of Mr. Brent and every member of the Keswick team.

The lovely guest rooms, gorgeous grounds, fine cuisine, special amenities, and exceptional service capped by "wow" moments – these elements set Keswick Hall apart. Whether guests come for a romantic getaway, a business meeting, a family reunion, a golf tournament, or a special event such as the February 2011 black tie gala benefiting the University of Virginia's Children's Hospital, they find the same outstanding elements. The holidays have always been festive and extravagant as well, from the popular Easter and Mother's Day brunches that have outdone one another time and again to the themed New Year's celebrations with spectacular fireworks. To ring in 2003, for example, guests enjoyed an around-the-world, European-style house party in, as Michael Pownall described it, the "very big, very nice house" that is Keswick Hall. In 2008, a 1920s theme meant goldfish swimming in strategically located fishbowls and an impressive array of flappers skirting around the hotel. And then there's Christmas. One North Carolina family started coming for Christmas the first year the hotel was open, and has been coming ever since.

Christmas at Keswick – Year After Year

Anne and John Allen Cates, Tar Heel born and bred, came to Virginia to watch the University of North Carolina play the University of Virginia on October 23, 1993. After the game, the Cates had dinner with friends at a "new" place in town – Keswick Hall, which had opened that August. They liked it so much, they decided to come back for Christmas, and thus began a family tradition. The first year, there were "maybe ten other people at the hotel," recalled Mrs. Cates. "We felt like we owned the place."

During the nearly two decades the Cates have been coming to the hotel, they have seen a number of changes – major, minor, and in between: the dining room moved up one level, for example, and two pools and four tennis courts were added, the circular driveway went from gravel to cobblestone, and the portrait of the Boocock brothers moved from a first floor hallway to the third floor outside Room 35 to the Villa Crawford. The family has noticed more and more people joining the caroling on Christmas Eve, and at one point (they can't remember when) they began finding filled Christmas stockings on their pillows after the caroling. Their Christmas gift exchange and tea times always took place in the "drawing room" (or the "Jefferson room," as the Cates called it), now the library. No matter what has changed, "It still feels like an English country house," Mrs. Cates said. "We wouldn't be coming back year after year unless

The fireplace in the great hall has been a favorite spot for a Cates family photograph for 17 years. Here, in 2003, before Fossett's Restaurant was added, Anne and John Allen Cates stand with their two daughters, Ginny Cates Bowie (far left, next to her mother) and Catherine Cates (far right). The children of Ginny Cates Bowie and her husband Reverend Clyde Bowie (the unseen photographer) are (left to right around Granddad) Anne, Findley, and Parker. Note the curtains to the left where guests now find the entrance to Fossett's instead. (Photo courtesy of Catherine Cates.)

we loved it." She added that many aspects have always been consistent and perfect, including the *scones*. Daughter Catherine Cates said, "My dad loves to play golf. So we all have been to Scotland and have had a lot of scones around the world, but Keswick still has the best."

"Overall, Keswick has provided a wonderful Christmas environment for our family for 17 years," she added. "We all love the beautiful setting, the variety of activities, the outstanding decorations, and of course, those scones. People do a double take when I say we love going to

a hotel for Christmas, but Keswick is not 'just a hotel.' How could you stay away from a place that has five or six Christmas trees, fireplaces perfectly tended, and hot chocolate always at the ready? And a stocking on your pillow on Christmas Eve? Santa surely has Keswick firmly marked on his route."

Holly VandeWater, Keswick's revenue manager, has personally been taking Anne Cates' Christmas reservations for more than ten years. "Her pleasant southern accent can be recognized the moment she says hello!" she said. "It has been such a joy to watch her grandchildren grow up and go off to college, and maybe one day, we'll host a wedding for them."

Everything but Ordinary

A wedding true to Keswick form is a glorious wedding indeed. "Keswick is the best place ever to have a wedding," said Casi Conner, who married Jimmy Cottrell on October 2, 2010. "Having my wedding here was like Christmas morning," she said, "– full of surprises, everything but ordinary, everyone treated like kings and queens from start to end, and yet you feel right at home. Not only were we blessed with the perfect weather, but with perfect people around us. Keswick's staff made it that way, catering to our every need – truly a bride's dream. The friendly staff had treats for our two dogs, Lexi and Hayden, and took them on walks for us, and my future husband and the groomsmen enjoyed an afternoon of the finest golf on the east coast while all

Christmas at Keswick Hall is sometimes snowy and sometimes warm, but always festive and welcoming.

twelve of my bridesmaids got their hair and makeup done at the same time in one of the spacious rooms. Having this service available made it possible for our whole family to be together. I thought surely there was no way the whole evening would be flawless, but it was! From the four course dinner in my dream tent, to a customized bar, an evening of dancing, and a massive fireworks show overlooking the beautiful Keswick Estate and Blue Ridge Mountains, the staff made it happen.

"After we said good night to our friends and family, we opened the door and to our surprise, our room was cleaned again, and champagne and slices of our wedding cake were ready for us, along with a gorgeous imported cheese display. There were rose petals all over the room and bed! Talk about service! In the morning, despite all the late night activities, a wonderful brunch, fresh made-to-order omelets and choices beyond your imagination, were ready for our guests. Simply five star!" When Mr. and Mrs. James Merrill Cottrell returned to Keswick on their first visit back as husband and wife, "we were greeted with the same lovely smiles and service. We checked into our room and found two dog beds, food and water bowls waiting for Lexi and Hayden, a martini bowl full of dog treats, delicious cheese and crackers, Keswick wine, and a very personal note. It exceeded our expectations in every aspect! There is a strong sense of family at Keswick, and we will continue to come back because of this. We just can't get enough!"

Casi Conner, like so many Keswick brides before her, practically floated every step of the way down the Villa Crawford staircase on her way to the ceremony on the lower level terrace. (Photo courtesy of Patricia Lyons.)

Lynn Easton, president of Easton Events, a local company that has designed four or five weddings a year at Keswick Hall, confirmed the unique combination of quality, panache, and ambiance that guests experience at Keswick. "The greatest thing about it is that you really get to have a house party," she said. "The way it's set up, it's like going to a villa to have your wedding – the building itself has so much to offer. You can walk down the hall in your robe, but the staff will do everything in their power to make everything perfect. There are not many places on the east coast that are comparable to Keswick."

There is something unique about Keswick; it *is* "more of a home than a commercial enterprise," just as Sir Bernard Ashley intended. Keswick Hall is the kind of place where your dogs are as welcome and as pampered as you are and where the couches are so comfy they practically invite you to sit down or even take a nap, but at the same time, at every turn, you find incredible food, outstanding service, gorgeous antiques, and delightful surprises – a subtle and appealing duality that on the one hand sets guests at ease and on the other, serves them with the highest standards.

The "strong sense of family" that Casi Cottrell observed translates into an incredible team that makes it all happen – and not only where it is seen, but also where it is not. Lynn Easton has observed that every challenge is approached with the understanding that there is a solution, and this mentality has served the client, the planner, and the hotel staff very well. She recalled one guest who requested a 22-foot deciduous tree in full leaf as part of the wedding reception decor. It was to be cut for the occasion, hauled to the site, and installed inside the dinner tent. Getting the tree inside the tent was one thing, and getting it to stand in place was another, but the Easton Events staff worked together with the Keswick staff to make it happen as if there was no big deal about it. Another time, the client had insisted on specially made benches for his rustic-themed event, but had not given the go-ahead on the work soon enough to allow sufficient time for the varnish to dry. When someone sat down on a newly varnished bench just hours before the event and stood back up with stained pants, the staff knew they had to do something, and quickly. Everyone worked together to staple burlap to the seats from underneath, thereby enhancing the rustic theme of the event and keeping the guests from sticking to the varnish.

The orchestration of details that make a perfect event has been beautifully articulated by Wendy Nelson, director of private events, who makes a habit of sending applause by email to the entire Keswick team a day or so after the guests have gone home and the tables and chairs are again in their storage spaces. In her lively style, she gives insight into the complexities of the operation and recognizes the often unseen elements that make it work. One sample, following a wedding with 200 guests: "Well, it's Monday and once again we

Casi Conner and Jimmy Cottrell got married at Keswick Hall on October 2, 2010, amid family and close friends, and overlooking spectacular countryside. "Having my wedding here was a dream come true!" said the bride in retrospect. (Photos courtesy of Patricia Lyons.)

showed what a perfect job we do when we all pull together – a colossal thank you from us … to those who came through with muscle to move many many tables and chairs when we needed it. To the brilliant culinary team who made Caesar explosions for 200 and mini-cheeseburgers in the middle of the night – beautiful plates and seriously great attitudes – the food was perfect and lovely and we are so thankful you make it so easy for us!! To the always wonderful housekeeping department for sending us incredible help, and for helping clean up the giant mess – the hotel looks brand new today! To the front desk for keeping everyone moving, cars in order, coats hung up – all while answering phones and looking like movie stars. Have no idea how they do it! To our incredible amazing private events staff and Fossett's servers – tireless, organized, professional, did I say tireless? And all of them so good looking even after 13 hours – we could not have a better staff. To the bartenders who had their hands full and kept it going when it got crazy. To the cheerful morning staff who moved all the tables back into place at a time when most of the world is sleeping on Sunday morning!! And of course, to our fearless leader. Thank you, thank you all! I say it every time, but I am so proud to be a part of this team with all of you. We really are the best hotel in the country!!!"

No kidding. In October of 2010, Keswick Hall was named by *Condé Nast* the #1 small resort in mainland United States. Matthias Smith, general manager, sent employees individual hand-written congratulations cards saying he was "very appreciative of a very accomplished team" and inviting them each to come spend a night at "our little countryside gem" as a guest of the hotel. What better way for anyone to indulge in the elegance, to relax in the comfort, to bask in the sunshine, to soak in the history. If only Bob Crawford could see the Villa he built a hundred years earlier. Keswick Hall – indeed, how aptly affirmed "a dream come true."

The stage was set in 1912 when the Villa Crawford took its place on the Virginia landscape. Keswick Hall, grand and elegant, continues to be an extraordinary place to connect and reconnect with friends, family, or someone special any time of the year, and the perfect place to relax, to play, to explore, and to celebrate. Every day, memories are made here. (Photo, left, courtesy of Patricia Lyons; photo, above, by Philip Beaurline.)

Postscript

Reactions to *The Story of Keswick Hall* in the three years since its publication have been overwhelmingly positive, and interest in the history of this unique property continues to grow. Having a story turns out to be greatly appealing. Having one that's not linear and predictable, but instead has numerous ups and downs, unexpected elements, mysterious gaps, crazy characters and high drama, turns out to be a mirror of real life that many can identify with and find comfort in. Idiosyncrasies morph into assets; singularity and uniqueness drive interest.

As interest grows, information continues to emerge. Mrs. Crawford's nasty dog and how he met his untimely death, George Nelson's "brain fever" that led to Mary Ellen's pony, Gertrude Mitchell's courageous step into the oval pool, B.A.'s helicopter touching down on the newly seeded 18th green – these new stories and more have created a clearer picture of the whole and have given us enhanced windows into the world as it was. Of course the world as it is plays in as well. The continued daily comings and goings naturally become part of the next chapter, which already has several high points but cannot yet be compiled. Eight months post-publication, in January 2012, the Richmond, Virginia, based Riverstone Group added the property to its collection of luxury destinations. The purchase set a series of events and changes in motion, including festive centennial celebrations and a new Pete Dye golf course, which opened in September 2014. Called Full Cry, the course honors local heritage and infuses both the course and the entire enterprise with the drive, determination and energy that this foxhunting term suggests. The property's new name, Keswick Hall and Golf Club, reflects the passion and direction moving forward.

It is said that location is the only thing the new golf course has in common with the Arnold Palmer and Fred Findlay courses that preceded it. Yet location is critical. Location connects the property to the unchanging Southwest Mountains that frame it, to those who walked this piece of earth before us and made their mark, to the local community that lends character and charm, to the larger world that comes to visit. People, as always, are at the heart of its story. In an exceptional example of purposeful minds directing adaptive reuse, of forward motion and stamina despite inevitable bumps and setbacks, of traditions borrowed and reworked, of the value of authenticity reaffirmed, Keswick Hall continues to shine.

Acknowledgements

The best part of writing *The Story of Keswick Hall* was meeting and becoming better acquainted with many wonderful people who shared freely and happily and made the book not only possible, but also immensely richer. This story is their story.

Many people helped; some helped tremendously. My gratitude is huge and endless to Drew Machat for his infinite patience with infinite changes and additions to the text and for working yet one more authentic or enlightening image into the page layout; to Annette Owens for her cheerful willingness to edit skillfully through many revisions and for her excellent reader's perspective; to Nita Palermo for her incredible eye for detail, continual support, and boundless ideas; to Sam Towler for researching the convoluted history of ownership and control; to Sara Augustine for not giving up on me and for her genius with design; to Peter McDonough for documents, information, and good cheer; to the grown children of Donald Stevens (Rosely, Stewart, Nini, and Poppy) for kindly sharing their father's involvement and many newspaper clippings; to the family of Glenn Reynolds (Dottie, Tim, Dave and Bonnie) for mountains of useful information, photos, and support; to Rebecca Bell Nordin for jump-starting the Crawford research and providing much-needed early enthusiasm; to Jeanne & Ed Cusick for their gracious encouragement and advice; to Matthias Smith for saying yes; to Dan Abrashoff for stories, clarifications, and the perfect touch of nostalgia; to Lincoln Machat and Beth Peery for all their help wading through options and paperwork; to Samuel Machat and Sandy Yanos for holding down the fort; to Jen Fariello for the perfect cover photo; to Patricia Lyons, Jim Carpenter, Philip Beaurline, Andre Maier, and Ed Roseberry for sharing their outstanding professional photography; to Phyllis Koch for insight and the only photo of the "real" B.A.; and to Bob Reid for piquing my interest in the first place. Let me say here how very, very grateful I am to each of you.

My heartfelt thanks also extends to others who made the final product richer and better in their own way, whether through ideas, memories, photos, leads, documents, information, clarification, encouragement, enthusiasm, or expertise: Elisabeth Aaron, Yara Acker, Susan Allan, Tim & Suzanne Allard, Dean Andrews, David Ashley, Nick Ashley, Peggy Augustus, Chuck Baker, Edie Ballard, Cindy (Sowers) Barnes, Art Beltrone, Jim

Blake, Blandy Boocock, Bobby Bowers, Olivia Branch, Cary Brent, Lynne Brubaker, Elizabeth Bullock, Sandra Burke, Cheryl Butcher, Catherine Cates, John Cassagne, Don Celec, Avery Chenoweth, Casi Cottrell, Debbie Dabney, Alice Dalton, George & Linda Davies, Adam Donovan-Groves, Lynda Downey, Lynn Easton, Carrie & Jay Eisenberg, Laura Fekishazy, Colonel Lew Flanders, John Gaines III, Beverley & Gary Garbaccio, Paul Gaston, Maurice Gibbons, Debbie Gibbs, Kim Gibbs, Eric Gibson, Scott Goss, Jim Hall, Peter Hallock, Craig Hartman, Richard Hewitt, Nancy Holt, Anne Hooff, Jake Jacobson, Mairi Kincaid, Chuck & Susie Kincannon, Betsy Lang, Ruth Langhorne, Matthew Lawrence, K. Edward Lay, Richard Leake Jr., Buddy Leffers, Vicky Legg, Rose LeMaster, Amy Lewis, Mary Lewis, Casey Lockwood, Colette Long, Claudia Lynn, Mary Jo McCarrick, Eric McGraw, Vladimir Mednikov, Alfreda Melvin, Scott Meynig, Mike Miller, Harriet & Dan Mohler, Winkey Motley, Pat (Spicer) Napoleon, Wendy Nelson, Tom Nolan, Margaret O'Bryant, Bob Paxton, Liz Ratcliffe, Jenny Rector, George Reynolds, Hans Olav & Anna Greta Riddervold, Barclay Rives, Nancy Root, Jim Routson, Peter Sandman, Ginny Semmes, Holly Settle, Curtis Shaver, Emma (Ashley) Shuckburgh, Duane Snider, Sheridan Snyder, Al Suttle Jr., Jessica Thiele, Terri Thompson, Albert Turnbull, Joan (Florence) Tutan, Gordon Wheeler, Libby Wilson, Scott Wolfe, Martin Wood, and Andre Xavier.

Acknowledgements Addendum: The fascinating, complex story told on these pages has found its place and made its mark mostly because of numerous individuals who shared in the excitement and told others. Many expressed gladness that their own memories were now rooted in a bona fide documentation. Some added substance and made the rich story richer. Some played key roles in getting the story out. To each one who helped, I am exceedingly grateful. Avery Chenoweth, an outstanding local author, graciously and enthusiastically spread the word about the book: to the Library of Virginia, where it was nominated for a nonfiction award; to Tara Wheeler at Channel 19, who did a news story in June 2011; to Carol Troxell at New Dominion Bookshop, where a signing was held that first summer; to David Maurer, feature writer at the Daily Progress, who wrote a wonderful article in August 2011, affirmed the work and encouraged me more than he can know; and to Terri Allard, who put together a 12-minute segment for PBS's Charlottesville Inside Out which aired in April 2014. Peggy Weems, who as a child had met the elderly Mrs. Crawford (Greenough) and whose grandfather, George Eager, had been the boys' tutor, saw David

Maurer's article and generously offered invaluable insight, a necklace of silver beads that had belonged to Mrs. Crawford, and new photos and stories that added immensely to the frequently told Crawford piece; naturally, precious friendship developed. Mary Ellen Voci, grand-niece of Rose Nelson (owner of Villa Crawford, 1928-36), gladly answered many questions and shared her family's home movies from their time as residents. Martin McKie purchased the first copy as the shipment came off the truck, and Robert Linn sent heartfelt thanks for the copy he bought for his daughter Katie, who married at Keswick Hall in October 2012; Marty and Bob both thereby launched great friendships and have lent their support in countless ways. Dottie Reynolds and Rosely Stevens were unfailingly encouraging from our very first meetings. The book was also featured at a presentation called "If Buildings Could Talk" at the 2012 Virginia Festival of the Book, thanks to Cheryl Schwandt, friend and fellow tennis player, who hit the first ball in that winning point. Rick Butts, the first general manager under the new ownership, affirmed and promoted the value of the property's history in numerous ways; Monte Hansen, the second, followed suit with gusto. Jennifer Crisp, public relations manager at Keswick Hall, created a history page on the resort's web site, and linked it to Terri Allard's PBS segment. Jessica Turnbull Deale, granddaughter of Knox Turnbull, happened upon the site and the segment, and expressed tearful gratitude that the impact of her grandfather's courage had not been forgotten. She was proof of Dean Williams' wise words that people who document histories of special people, places and events are like those who plant trees: "The result is valued more by each future generation."

Huge thanks also to Drew Machat and Sara Augustine for their help with this second printing, to Bradley Machat and Lisa Decker for continually talking up the story with guests at the hotel, to Jason Rethemeyer for his expertise with the old home movies, to Chris Samley for walking me through, to John Reyburn for encouraging me to keep going, and to my parents, Barbara and Ray Castelli, for their love from the beginning.

Time Line

March 27, 1911	Robert B. Crawford purchased 134 acres in Keswick for $10,000 and contracted with Eugene Bradbury to design an Italianate villa.
1912	Bob Crawford and his wife, L. Florence Olney Crawford, moved into the **Villa Crawford**; 8000-square-foot home cost $100,000 to build.
August 12, 1913	Bob Crawford purchased the adjacent, 181-acre Broad Oak farm for $7500.
December 9, 1917	Bob Crawford conveyed the property to his wife.
September 1918	Bob Crawford moved to Baltimore.
June 1919	L. Florence Olney Crawford secured a divorce in Reno.
October 5, 1919	Bob Crawford found dead in Baltimore.
October 12, 1919	L. Florence Olney Crawford married H.W. Greenough.
July 3, 1923	L. Florence Olney Greenough sold the **Villa Crawford** to Leighton Kramer for $50,000.
March 26, 1928	Leighton Kramer sold the **Villa Crawford** to Dr. Ridgely F. and Mabel G. Hanscom for $38,500.
September 10, 1928	Dr. and Mrs. Hanscom sold the **Villa Crawford** to George E. and Rose L. Nelson for $44,000.

June 29, 1936	Rose L. Nelson sold the **Villa Crawford** to Maria W. Heid for $30,000 (this was thought a fair price during the Depression).
July 25, 1947	Maria W. and August Heid sold the **Villa Crawford** to the Keswick Corporation for $50,000.
September 1947	Keswick Corporation purchased additional acreage, including R.O. Hall's adjacent 127-acre Paradise Farm, gaining access to Route 250, and contracted with Fred Findlay to design the golf course.
New Year's Day 1948	Formal opening of the **Keswick Country Club**; 1500 people attended.
July 1948	Formal opening of the tennis courts; exhibition match with national tennis stars.
May 30, 1949	Formal opening of the oval, steel pool; exhibition by Olympic diving champion.
June 15, 1949	Formal opening of the golf course.
1949	Keswick Corporation purchased 25 additional acres from Chesapeake & Ohio Railroad when the tracks were realigned.
July 21, 1951	"Aqua Maids in Review" swim ballet.
January 11, 1953	Tragic plane crash on property; three men died.
June 30, 1955	Keswick Cavalier Corporation (Sidney Banks) purchased the majority of Keswick Corporation stock; renamed property the **Country Club of Keswick.**
Summer 1955	*Giant*, starring Elizabeth Taylor and Rock Hudson, was filmed in Keswick.
September 1955	Work "underway" on the back nine holes of the golf course; completed by spring of 1956.
November 10, 1960	Al Suttle bid $160,000 on the **Country Club of Keswick** and assumed the operation.
1961	Club sold 21.5 acres to Commonwealth of Virginia for Interstate 64, losing access to Route 250.
1965	Knox Turnbull took over, changed name to **Keswick Club of Virginia**.
Summer 1967	Three more tennis courts opened.
Summer 1969	Virginia State Open Golf Championship; five-lane Olympic-length pool opened.
Summer 1970	Virginia State Open Golf Championship; space bubble erected over five-lane pool.

Winter 1971	Space bubble erected over three of the tennis courts.
September 7, 1971	Knox Turnbull died.
July 1972	**Keswick Club of Virginia** folded.
1973-1977	Golf course and 19th Hole tavern alone remained operational as leased entities.
1977	Golf pro Belden MacMillan was murdered in the club's front parking lot; crime remains unsolved.
1977-1979	Bill Lane attempted to remake the property into a vineyard resort.
March 1980	*The Four Seasons* starring Alan Alda and Carol Burnett filmed in the **Villa Crawford**.
May 7, 1980	**Keswick Club** reopened under the direction of Glenn & Dottie Reynolds.
April 1981	William Burress purchased the property.
Fall 1982	**Keswick Club** closed.
July 1984	William Burress sold the property to George O'Brien for $1.5 million; O'Brien set up a partnership with Thomas Curtis.
December 1985	George O'Brien sold his share to Thomas Curtis, who contracted with Arnold Palmer to redesign the golf course.
Early 1990	Thomas Curtis owed $18 million to 30 creditors.
April 9, 1990	An offer to purchase the property out of bankruptcy came from the Keswick Acquisition Corporation, representing Sir Bernard Ashley.
September 17, 1990	Sir Bernard Ashley officially purchased the property for $5.5 million; property became **Keswick Hall, Club & Estate**.
September 23, 1992	**Keswick Club** opened, including indoor-outdoor pool, three clay tennis courts, and golf course redesigned by Arnold Palmer.
August 1993	**Keswick Hall** opened as a 48-room "country house hotel."
Summer 1997	"The Hideaway" opened (later called the Pavilion, and now the Tennis & Aquatic Center), including pool and two tennis courts.

May 6, 1999	Sir Bernard Ashley sold **Keswick Hall, Club & Estate** to Orient-Express for $13.5 million.
December 17, 2002	Audubon certification achieved for the golf course.
Summer 2003	Horizon pool opened.
June 2004	"Fossett's" restaurant opened.
Spring 2010	"Courtside Vineyard" planted.
October 2010	*Condé Nast* named **Keswick Hall** the #1 small resort in mainland United States; two new tennis courts added.
March 2011	One hundred years since Bob Crawford purchased this property; fine dining wine cellar "Treble" opened.
2012	**Villa Crawford** is 100 years old! In January of this year, Keswick Hall & Club is sold to the Riverstone Group for more than $20 million.
September 16, 2014	New Pete Dye golf course *Full Cry* opened.

Notes

page 13

The first item on the Chain of Title housed at the Charlottesville Albemarle Historical Society, which later includes Robert B. Crawford's purchase of Keswick land, is Rogers v. Rogers heirs, entered March 3, 1840. Robert B. Crawford purchased 134 acres in 1911 from "Bessie Tucker Fellowes and husband Edward H," recorded in Deed Book 145, page 418. The land was noted as being part of the Ingleside tract, and purchased by Crawford after numerous previous transactions over the years. It was described in Item XVI in the Chain of Title as follows:

> "[Plat 422] shows 134 acres, beingning [sic] at stake on Charlottesville Road, thence along center of roat [sic] 122 74/100 poles, thence leaving road S 24 ¼ W 35 po [sic] to stake, thence with Smith and with Everett estate S 14 ¼ E 119 po to post, thence with Hughes and Meade N 63 ¼ E 167 4/10 po to western gate post of Meade road, and along west side of Meade road N 23 ¼ W140 9/10 po to the beginning."

page 21

The full introductory text of the description of Broad Oak from Edward Mead's *Historic Homes of the South-West Mountains Virginia* (1898):

> If the lover of antique, who delights in old moss-covered buildings, whose every plank, shingle and nail tells the tale of a past century, when building was done under such difficulties by the early settlers, then the Broad Oak house, when first entered in 1861 by its present proprietor, would have rejoiced the heart, and called forth from a pathetic nature a pathetic ode. When or by whom the first little one-storied house, having but two rooms, was built is beyond the knowledge of any one now living. A few feet from its door stood a giant oak, from which it takes its name; it measures twenty feet in circumference at the base, and spreads a shade over the yard of more than eighty feet in diameter each way as if in protection of its peaceful occupants, and has sheltered 'neath its dense foliage many

generations. This monarch of the forest has been known to the community for its conspicuous size and beauty since the recollection of the oldest inhabitant, who speak of it as being nearly as large a tree in their youth as now. The indications of its extreme age are now manifest, and this patriarch of the original forest is gradually failing in strength, as shown by its decaying limbs and withering leaves; yet it still forms in its graceful old age a particular and striking object, being one of the few familiar landmarks of this historic region. Three more oaks, nearly as large, also stand in the rear of the house, one of which was struck by lightning in 1888 and immediately died. Stepping into the house, the first object to strike the visitor's notice is its rough floor of wide plank, without tongue or groove, and nailed with large wrought nails from a common forge; its shingles were moss-covered, and put on with similar nails; its chimney was half stone and half brick, the latter being much larger in size than the present kind. Its huge framing timbers measured twelve by fourteen inches for the sills, and four by eight for the sleepers and joists, all being hewed by hand, and as sound as when put in. The cellar and foundation walls were of stone, fourteen inches thick, and cemented with mud mortar. The one largest room was sixteen feet square, while the little garret room were mere cubby-holes, in which one could scarcely stand erect. Such was the first house at Broad Oak. About 1840 an addition was made by a two-story room joined to this old part, and in 1874 the old part was raised another story to correspond with it, placing all under one roof, as shown in the engraving. There are other evidences which tend to establish the very early settlement of Broad Oak. Immediately in front of the house (as was the superstitious custom in those days) was the remains of an old graveyard, but without any headstones. A few feet from the front door also showed the site of a well, but tradition says that its waters were so bitter with mineral that it was filled up, under the belief of being a judgment for having been placed so near the graveyard.... But the strongest proof of evidence of its being settled early in the eighteenth century is that of a Colonial penny being ploughed up near the dwelling in 1863. This penny has on one side a shield, upon which are quartered the arms of England, Scotland, and Virginia, the whole encircled with the word "Virginia, 1773;" on the reverse side was a head with the words "Georgius III. Rex." This proves the origin of the term "Old Dominion," Virginia being thus acknowledged a part of England in gratitude for her loyalty.

page 23

The *Charlottesville Daily Progress* article regarding Bob Crawford's death appeared on the front page, far left column, on Monday Afternoon, October 6, 1919. It continued as follows:

"As is his custom every Sunday morning, Carl Bunting, manager of the Inn, went to serve Crawford breakfast in his room. Bunting opened the door to find him dead in bed. Crawford, according to Bunting, appeared in the best of health when he retired shortly after 9 o'clock last night.

"Crawford is said to own a mansion and considerable property in Charlottesville, although he has made his home at the Inn for the past year. Efforts are being made to communicate with the dead man's sister in Washington, D.C.

"... While a student at the University of Virginia he met Mrs. L. Florence Olney, the divorced wife of a resident of New

England, who had resumed her mother's name of Olney, and their marriage followed. Soon after the wedding they went to the fashionable Keswick neighborhood, in this county, and built a palatial home..."

The property that Robert B. Crawford conveyed to his wife on December 19, 1917, included the original 134 acres (D.B. 166, p. 393), the 181 acres acquired from Edward C. Mead (D.B. 152, p. 249), and a tract of ¼ acre acquired from Washington Braxton (D.B. 146, p. 173).

page 24

The *Charlottesville Daily Progress* article regarding Mrs. Crawford's remarriage appeared on the front page, far left column, on Thursday Afternoon, October 16, 1919. In the third column appeared a list of "THREE DIVORCES GRANTED." Clearly it was possible to obtain a divorce in Virginia. It is unknown why Mrs. Crawford traveled to Reno to secure hers.

page 33

Edward Mead's *Historic Homes of the South-West Mountains Virginia* (1898) also provides a glimpse of the town of Keswick at the turn of the twentieth century:

> "Keswick has risen to a place of some importance. It now contains a large brick depot and reception room, three stores, with several shops, drug-store, and telephone connection with Charlottesville and other points."

page 37

The *Charlottesville Daily Progress* article regarding the "Gala Opening" of the new Keswick pool appeared on Tuesday Afternoon, May 31, 1949. The accompanying photo of Donald Stevens awarding the winner's cup did not reproduce well. The article states:

> "The Keswick Country Club had a gala day yesterday at the opening of its new swimming pool. There were 25 contestants for the "Miss Keswick" title, of whom about ten appeared to parade for the judges. These were Miss Lollie Carruthers, Miss Phillipa Stanwood, Miss Pat Wingfield, Miss Jon Florence, Miss Pat Hawkins, Miss Meta Stuart Todd, Miss Mary Jarman, Miss Joan Grimes, and Miss Danny Nichols, who won first place.
>
> "The Charlottesville Municipal Band played during the supper hour, when the club served a buffet supper for those who attended. Devon, an entertainer from Washington, played his accordion, and accompanied himself on the piano, from 7 until 11 P.M."

page 38

It is unclear how 1939 came to be erroneously associated with the opening of the Keswick golf course. Following are sections of newspaper articles from 1947-49 to erase any doubt.

> "Keswick Estate Purchased As New Country Club Site: 'Villa Crawford,' the August Heid estate at Keswick, has been selected for development as a new country club for Albemarle and neighoring counties. A group of local citizens and residents of the county

exercised an option to purchase the property on Saturday. The purchasing group was organized by Donald G. Stevens, who will direct plans for the development of the estate.... Outside improvements will include installation of tennis and swimming facilities, and in the ultimate plan the building of an 18-hole golf course, to be designed by a nationally known golf architect." *Charlottesville Daily Progress*, Charlottesville, VA., Monday Afternoon, July 21, 1947

"Heid Estate Prospective Country Club: A group of city and county residents, headed by Donald G. Stevens, has exercised an option for the purchase of 'Villa Crawford,' the August Heid estate at Keswick, and will develop the 300-acre property into a new country club for residents of this area, it was disclosed yesterday....Outside improvements will include installation of tennis and swimming facilities, and the ultimate laying out of an 18-hole golf course." *Charlottesville News Leader*, July 22, 1947

"Charter Granted to Country Club: Keswick Corporation's Directors Are Listed: A charter was granted yesterday by the State Corporation Commission to the Keswick Corporation to operate a country club at 'Villa Crawford,' the former August Heid estate at Keswick which was purchased by a local syndicate last Saturday....Eventually, it is anticipated that an 18-hole golf course will be included in the development of the property...." *Charlottesville Daily Progress*, Charlottesville, VA., Saturday Afternoon, July 26, 1947

"Fred Findlay to Map Layout of Keswick Course: Donald G. Stevens, president of the new Keswick Country Club, announced today that Fred Findlay, nationally known golf architect, has been selected to make the layout of an 18-hole golf course to be constructed on the property of the Keswick Corporation...." *Charlottesville Daily Progress*, Charlottesville, VA., Wednesday Afternoon, August 27, 1947

"Keswick Club's Opening Set for New Year's Day: Formal opening of the new Keswick Country Club has been set for January 1, when a buffet supper will be given for the members, it was announced today by Donald G. Stevens, club president....Work on the club's golf course is to start this fall and will probably take 18 months to complete...." *Charlottesville Daily Progress*, Charlottesville, VA., Saturday Afternoon, August 30, 1947

"New Club Buys R.O. Hall Farm: Keswick Corporation Now Has 527 Acres: The Keswick Corporation has purchased the 127-acre "Paradise Farm," on Route 20, from R.O. Hall, bringing the total acreage to be developed as the new Keswick Country Club to 527 acres, it was announced today by Donald G. Stevens, club president....Fred Findlay, golf course architect, is already at work on the layout of the club's 18-hole golf course, on which construction will be started this fall...." *Charlottesville Daily Progress*, Charlottesville, VA., Friday Afternoon, September 19, 1947

"Club to Begin Full Operation at Charlottesville February 16: Officers of the Keswick Corporation announced today that the Keswick Country Club would begin full operation on Monday, February 16, at which time the dining room, cocktail lounge, and other club house facilities will be open to members. The Keswick Club had its formal opening on New Year's Day, which was attended by more than 1,500 persons, including most of its 350 resident members, their families and guests....Mr. Stevens also stated that the first nine holes of a projected 18-hole golf course are not scheduled for completion until the Spring of 1949. It will require most of this year to prepare the fairways and greens for seeding, although much clearing has been done and a nursery for the sodding of greens is planted already, it was pointed out...." *Richmond Times Dispatch*, February 7, 1948

"Carolinian Named Keswick Golf Pro: Tommy Card, 32-year-old Raleigh, N.C., professional, has been named to take charge of the golf activities at the Keswick Country Club, beginning May 1, it was announced today by the club's president, Donald G. Stevens.... The Keswick Country Club will formally open its golf course on June 1." *Charlottesville Daily Progress*, Charlottesville, VA., Thursday Afternoon, March 10, 1949

"Keswick Golf Course Will Open Tomorrow: The new 9-hole Keswick Country Club golf course will open for members and their guests tomorrow. An exhibition match is scheduled for Saturday afternoon. Meeting in the 18-hole exhibition will be John S. Battle, Jr., Walter Hagen, Jr., of Richmond, Art Deering, Farmington professional, and Tommy Card, Keswick pro." *Charlottesville Daily Progress*, Charlottesville, VA., Tuesday Afternoon, June 14, 1949

page 54

The convoluted pattern of ownership and control of the club during the late 1950s and early 1960s is only somewhat clarified by a study of deed book records. The corporations that owned the property changed names, merged with each other, or both; some of the people in prominent positions within these corporations held different positions of leadership during different phases; and pieces of the property were sold and new parcels (large and small) were purchased during and alongside the changes in ownership. Every effort has been made to be clear and accurate, but it is acknowledged that important components may be missing or mistaken.

page 71

Numerous attempts were made to substantiate the exhibition tennis matches played at Keswick by Arthur Ashe and Billy Jean King during the late 1960s. In the end no documentation was found, but various club members who were there at the time, including Dottie Reynolds and Professor Paul Gaston, clearly remember both of these top players coming to the Keswick Club for these matches.

page 91

The Avery Chenoweth quote is from the *Charlottesville/Albemarle Business Observer Magazine* of May 28-June 3, 1992.

(throughout the book) *Charlottesville Daily Progress* and *Daily Progress* are the same publication.

Sources

The material used in preparing this book came mainly from interviews with many people who lived through the events described in the book – from their own memories and scrapbooks and photo albums – as well as from many newspaper clippings, written reflections, magazine articles, personal and business correspondence, club newsletters, the University of Virginia Special Collections Library, and the sources listed below. Orient-Express graciously and generously allowed use of their image library, as did the professionals also listed here.

The 100 Year History of The Keswick Hunt Club, Barclay Rives, 1996

Albemarle: Jefferson's County 1727-1976, John Hammond Moore, University Press of Virginia, 1976

Albemarle & Charlottesville: An Illustrated History of the First 150 Years, Rick Britton, Historical Publishing Network, San Antonio, Texas, 2006

Archie and Amelie: Love and Madness in the Gilded Age, Donna M. Lucey, Three Rivers Press, 2007

The Architecture of Jefferson Country, K. Edward Lay, University Press of Virginia, 2000

Barboursville Vineyards: Crafting Great Wines Inspired by Spirits of the Past, Chiles T.A. Larson, Barboursville Vineyards, 2008

Coming of Age in Utopia, The Odyssey of an Idea: Paul M. Gaston, NewSouth Books, Montgomery, 2010

Historic Virginia, Roy Wheeler, 1949

Laura Ashley, Martin Wood, Frances Lincoln Limited, 2009

Laura Ashley at Home, Nick Ashley, Fayal Greene, Catherine Haig, Susan Irvine, Paula Rice Jackson, Harmony Books, 1988

N&W Giant of Steam, Major Lewis Ingles Jeffries, Pruett Publishing Co., 1980

The Romance of Country Inns, Elizabeth Bond, Todtri Publications Inc., 1996

Saving Monticello, Marc Leepson, University of Virginia Press, 2001

Virginia Wine Country III, Hilde Gabriel Lee and Allan E. Lee, Hildesigns Press, Keswick, Virginia, 2004

Philip Beaurline (Photography): www.beaurline.com

Jim Carpenter (Gitchell's Studio): www.gitchellsstudio.com

Jen Fariello Photography: www.jenfariello.com

Phyllis Koch, A.S.I.D. Interior Design: www.phylliskochasid.com

Patricia Lyons Photography: patricia@patricialyonsphotography.com

Andre Maier Photography: www.andremaier.com

Ed Roseberry (Photography): Charlottesville, Virginia

Vaughn Images, Vaughn Media Inc.: www.joevaughn.com

Keswick Hall Index

上品、快適

exquisite

relaxing, peaceful
and everything that
I had hope and dreamed
see you again :)

Inspirational!

a gift indeed!

Elegant

Delightful

Great place!

It was wonderful!
Can't wait to come back.

Heavenly!

Looking forward to
a prompt return.

Fabulous!

Great Food!
Beautiful
place!

We loved it!

We'll be back!

"muy bien"

Exceptional!

Perfect

Beautiful!

Wonderful!!

Very nice, very welcoming
& friendly staff.

Beautiful! So relaxing
and peaceful See you again!

Charming.

Nice!!

Wunderbar!

So Wonderful!

Stunning!

Lovely, as always!

有難うございます。

Out of this world!

As Great As the
Pay was HOT!

bardo dobre

More than we imagined!

Breathtaking

Hard to Beat!